Strategies

.... The Magic Key

Ken Keacher

Dedicated with love to my family and friends

Strategies

.... The Magic Key

Written by Ken Keacher

Edited by Lynn Cross

Contact info and more at; strategybook.org

Acknowledgments

Foremost I want to acknowledge my family for everything, from supporting the commitment in both time and effort to develop the material for this project from proofreading, evaluating ideas and sharing in the myriad of challenges and triumphs that made up this process.

Second I want to acknowledge the amazing direct contributors to this project
Lynn Cross editor
Hugh Benowitz front cover illustration
Michael Beachy, interior illustrations and rear cover.

*Contributors BIOS and contact information available in the back of the book.

Recognition and thanks for additional insight, suggestions and collaboration from Robbins Madane's Training (RMT) staff and students.
Priscilla Arafat, David Block, Janis Cohen, Jeff Forte, Todd Gray, Cloe Madanes, Mark Peysha, Karen Rothstein, Melvin Waller. A huge, special thanks to Mr. Anthony Robbins.

Table of contents

The fable of the gatekeeper (a tale of two minds)

Author Introduction

The Fable of the Gatekeeper

It seems as though we are born into this world with an inner knowledge about a powerful place within ourselves—a place that we were told is outside of our consciousness and beyond our ability to understand. A place hidden behind a locked and guarded door that separates us from a truth we can feel, but cannot see. It is from this place that the elusive reason behind the reasons we do things springs forth, teasing our consciousness on rare occasions, like a glimpse of a fleeting reflection in a revolving door.

Try as we will to grasp its infinite power, to find the greater meaning, direction, and purpose in our lives, we are thrown back to our conscious mind. There, in our everyday consciousness, we run a labyrinth of clues to our behaviors, values, wishes, and desires. No matter how much we seek to understand this powerful place, we find we are no closer to unlocking the great mystery.

Yet, even in consciousness, each of us knows there are things in our heart that are true. We know that there is a point at which we are willing to take a stand, to affirm our own strategy. To remain true to our convictions without regard to even our own peril. To defend our actions against all forms of logic or reason that oppose us. These elusive reasons or strategies that, at their best, would lead us to sacrifice ourselves for the love of others.

These same strategies, at their worst, would sever ties with those who love us and cause us to approve of and engage in behavior destructive to ourselves and others. In our stubborn blindness, such trust in our strategies justifies our going down with the ship while standing firm on some meaningless point, even though doing so ends a relationship or allows us to slowly kill ourselves with deadly vices.

What possibilities might await us if by chance the great gate-keeper of the unknown slept? What would we learn if we were to seize that opportunity to unlock the door and gaze inside? Would we smile with the pleasant realization that there is no *unknowable*, there is only the *known* and the presently *unknown*? Would we then see clearly the simple order to the processes that direct our heart and mind? Could we appreciate those distinctions between our identity, our behavior, our needs as humans, and the ways in which we satisfy those needs? Would we see that the solution to the great mystery of our power and commitment was merely an understanding of the way we tie these things together for our benefit or peril? In other words. . . . .

a superior strategy

Author Introduction

It is often said that *"love makes us do strange things"*

Like most of us, all my life I've heard people saying this or that about their emotional needs. With couples we hear comments like "he only thinks of himself and doesn't care about my needs." What's really interesting is that while we may know there is a truth and a deeper meaning to those types of statements, I do not believe that it really means people are uncaring. Maybe more accurate is that most of us just don't know exactly what these *needs* are or have any understanding of how they work or tie together in our overall lives.

We do want to understand. Useful exploration of needs like love and purpose have struck a cord of universal interest with philosophers, deep thinkers and the rest of us throughout history. Huge amounts of information have been compiled over the years, especially in the last few centuries. Still, for the most part much of this information is unknown or has no practical application. Seemingly we have raised more questions than we have answered and people are no more fulfilled now than before.

Today the need for communication, understanding and the ability to maintain deep meaningful relationships with ourselves and others, is at an all-time high. In this book, I have set out to tie together these treasures of our past left us by forward thinking people from history who were ahead of their time. For me, this had to be done in a useful way, not only to clarify, but also to create understanding with practical use.

My unique perspective on this comes from developing an intimate understanding of our needs while spending four years speaking with people from all backgrounds on crisis and suicide lines. What I learned is that we all experience similar emotional desires and we share the same predictors for whether we feel fulfilled, or suicidal. Whether we have strong relationships or experience pain from not being able to meaningfully connect with others.

I have developed a simple concept for tying together our needs with a tool for understanding them that anyone can use. From casual relationships like sales, to important family or business relationships. This tool makes you immediately recognize the needs that are important to you and others, along with the ability to understand and shift how we satisfy them (the strategy). While this is a huge benefit, if only to improve your own life. For me, the greatest advantage and benefit is; to have a real tool of understanding for those difficult times when you absolutely must make a critical difference in the lives of those who you care about most.

When you think about it, it is almost guaranteed that at one time or another an important family member, a child, our partner, parent or friend will be in the midst of some emotional turmoil or faced with heartbreaking decisions. When that happens, this core strategy tool will help you to be the one who can make a meaningful difference and change lives for the better.

This strategies concept is now being used successfully by several top therapists, highly specialized personal development and relationship coaches and real people in every situation. It is fresh, exciting and its broad uses are still being discovered.

I am delighted when people share with me how these ideas have helped them. Of the benefits, I think it is great that so many people say that they have a renewed sense that they can finally relax and, "just be themselves" knowing for certain they will be successful. I believe that fulfills the following of our deepest emotional needs.

"We all want and deserve to be loved just for being ourselves."

Thank you for joining me, I'm very excited to share *Strategies, The Magic Key* with you now.   So let's go!

Ken

Chapter 1

The Strategy Within

As a young man I had always considered myself successful, even though my parents never had what you would call an abundance mentality. That didn't stop me. Looking back, it's probably what encouraged me to pay attention to finances and begin work at an early age. By age 17 I had saved up and owned three cars, and at age 19 I bought my first rental property. In my twenties, I had great friends and I was being mentored by one of, if not the most creatively brilliant and successful entrepreneurs in my part of the country. I was doing well in so many areas, and my parents were proud.

By the time I reached my thirties, people started asking me for advice on how they could be successful too. While I knew what I was doing that made me successful, that knowledge didn't seem to apply or translate well to others, and that made me wonder why not. With curiosity and determination to serve others, I decided to intensify my personal development studies to learn what, if any, universal characteristics would lead to someone's ability to succeed (something I had been interested in and studying all along anyway). I dug increasingly into the best available information and research on successes, such as Napoleon Hill's book *Think and Grow Rich,* in which he examined 500 super-successful people in the early 1900s, people like Andrew Carnegie, Henry Ford, and Thomas Edison. I also studied tons of business/sales psychology and general psychology, along with ideas from people like Deepak Chopra, Earl Nightingale, and Anthony Robbins. Anthony Robbins intrigued me with his use of NLP and human needs psychology, and so I spent several more years researching, actively studying, and following the origins of psychology, general semantics, hypnosis, and NLP, intently researching back to the 1700s in many cases.

In 2002 Tony Robbins teamed up with the respected family therapist Cloe Madanes. Together they began making videos of Strategic Interventions at his seminars in which he used human needs psychology (the idea that our behavior is an attempt to satisfy needs). I was deeply curious about programs like this and was one of the first people to get my hands on these films. In them, Tony was masterful at helping people come to terms with the real challenges in their lives and simultaneously design a compelling future for themselves in areas in which they had been blocked for years.

To me this seemed to be the universal understanding that I had been looking for. For the next four or five years (just as I do today) I continued to actively study Tony's use of various styles, along with the work of the renowned relationship researcher and expert from Washington State University, Dr. John Gottman. I also began taking calls on local crisis lines and the national suicide line. There, I could put this information to its absolute best use helping people. It also provided an excellent environment to see which of these philosophies and principles worked in the toughest of real-life situations.

I soon found that there's an interesting dynamic in psychology or change work that gives its practitioners the most trouble. The challenge is that no matter how good the advice is that someone is given, there's a good chance it will be rejected. In these cases, the client is said to be "resistant." They will say things like, "I know, but . . ." "I tried that, it didn't work." "I can't do that." "You don't understand my situation." Resistance to change is perhaps the largest and most slippery obstacle in helping people who are at their most desperate.

On some level, resistance is the only problem. Putting it simply, if you gave people general information on more empowering behaviors during their stay at treatment or rehab facilities, and if those recommendations were accepted and implemented, there would be no cases of relapse. Relapses affirm the existence of resistance to general information alone. Not that we necessarily need that sort of proof, as all of us have tried to help someone who wanted help but just didn't want to hear any advice, no matter how good the advice was.

Therapeutically, there are effective ways of dealing with resistance. One generally accepted method of helping someone beyond their own resistance is what is called "leverage." Leverage is based on something that the conflicted person places a higher value on, and by focusing on that, they can take the new advice to get the higher valued outcome. Here is an example of leverage being used with someone who resists giving up smoking. You would find something they value much more than smoking, such as being present for their grandchildren's births, birthdays, and graduations, and get them to focus intently on that higher value desire, then they may lower their resistance and be more receptive to receiving help and using good general advice.

Client resistance gave me real trouble. I decided to make this a central focus. Fortunately I had a good attitude, patience, and a lot of time. Sometimes, even with a good attitude, I found it very frustrating that people in desperate situations would cling to something and resist change even when, by their own admission, their alternatives were downright horrible. Then one day, after thousands of days of trying to put it together, it hit me. Everything came together, all my thoughts about what resistance is and why people resist. It is so simple and so embedded in us that it seems we are blind to it.

What I realized was that everyone was clinging to the same thing, not only the people in some sort of crisis. It was more than that; it was everybody, and they were doing it all the time. I started snooping into the lives of everyone I knew and in every kind of situation to see if it was universal, and it seemed to be. I could not find a person or situation where this truth did not stand, and as of today, I still have not. While "resistance" is a valid way to describe what people are doing, I think it draws our attention away from something else that is going on. People are not only resisting change. A better description may be that they are doing the opposite. They are clinging (for dear life in some cases) to something. They are clinging to a universal unconscious strategy, guideline, or idea of *how they believe they need to be.*

They are clinging to their choice of actions, and it doesn't matter if the results are positive or negative. They do not want to change, because of their inner conviction that justifies the behavior. People are clinging to drug use or to some particular pattern like being a workaholic or a carefree dropout or any number of descriptions. Whatever they believe their strategy is, they cling to it. Each person's core strategy is unique to them, like a fingerprint or a key, except it is not likely that we are born with our strategies. They seem to develop through our experience and conditioning from a very early age. Strategies can change and evolve, or they can become stuck, leaving the person in discord with their environment as they grow through different stages of life.

The term "clinging" best describes what people do when their strategy and circumstances give them emotional difficulty. At other times, when their strategy and environmental conditions are meeting their emotional needs, it might be better said that they "hold firm" to their strategy.

What I had noticed is what I would call a basic human need, that is to say, a universal emotional target that affects our behavior. I call it our "core strategy." It is that thing that we hold firm or cling to that tells us (by our conditioning) how we need to be. It is a necessity for us to believe that we know what we are doing, regardless of whether our lives are working well or not, and we will not change unless we are convinced at the level of our core strategy.

You may be thinking, that's not true always, there are plenty of people who admit that they are unhappy, that they do not know what to do and they want help. I understand that position. I worked with many people in that particular group. I'm saying that if their issues seem unresolvable, it is likely because these people will not give up that unhelpful position, for no other reason than that it is tied to the strategy they are clinging to and has nothing to do with actual circumstances or their ability.

I would even defend these people as being accurate. People would gladly change if they knew what to do. They would stop using drugs or they would repair their relationships. The challenge is that the advice they receive is not at the level of their strategy. It is only at the level of generally good advice. General advice does not help, because almost everyone knows they should not use drugs or they should get out of that bad relationship, and they should exercise and spend more time with their family. The advice has to be specific relative to their strategy itself to truly be accepted.

If we fail to recognize exactly how strong the need is for people to believe in the correctness of their strategy, we have trouble understanding or rationalizing this type of behavior. By calling it resistance, we have a tendency to place labels on it such as stubbornness, ego, or fear. Yet these classifications do not help us solve the issues and usually further contribute to our own belief that others are beyond help.

I believe the intention of a persons core strategy is always positive. When we affirm and align with a person's core strategy for satisfying their emotional needs (preferably with leverage), what was seen as general advice is now targeted to a deeper level, where it can accepted as their own. Remember, we all have a core strategy, and for the most part, our strategies are fantastic. They create the boundaries from which we hold our highest identities, serving beyond ourselves with a commitment unknown to anyone but ourselves. This is what people are clinging or holding firm to.

This something that we cling to has never been named before, yet all top therapists, parents and grandparents, or anyone else who has helped someone change has either intuitively or accidentally helped others make a change at this core level of strategy. My hope is to allow everybody to understand how personally we take our strategies and be enabled to use this simple tool consciously and deliberately, helping others without the time or perils of learning it intuitively.

I understand I'm introducing some new ideas, and of course new ideas need reasons to become accepted. In the following pages I will lay out and clarify how and why strategies work, based on real-life situations. I will also introduce a few more equally strong ideas about the reasons behind our behavior for you to consider. If nothing else, I promise considering these things will make our time together valuable. Beyond that, I will expand upon general human needs frameworks like Abraham Maslow and Anthony Robbins in a way never before offered, including distinctions between emotions and thought. New concepts based on my own original perspective that I have taken great care to be consistent with the RMT training philosophy I received studying directly with Cloe Madanes. Together you and I will travel through the needs in a simple way that will clarify some extremely empowering concepts that you can easily accept, if you choose, and thereby understand and supercharge your own strategy.

Chapter 2

When Strategies Fail

It was an extremely cold January in the late 1970s. I was living in the Upper Midwest City of Minneapolis, Minnesota. Temperatures in this part of the country during the winter months can fall below freezing for days, weeks, or even months on end. In this region, to say that it is extremely cold means life-threatening temperatures and bitter wind chills that penetrate one's very bones.

I was seventeen, and had just two weeks earlier moved across town with my mother and her new husband into a very modest home set on a corner of an established residential neighborhood. It was a one-story, two-bedroom bungalow with a full basement. The neighborhood was alive with neatly landscaped, stucco-covered homes much like ours or maybe a little larger, built in the 1930s by the sons of Minnesota's most promising early immigrants. Within walking distance were all the normal amenities of such a neighborhood in that era: a post office, drugstore, café, and a mid-sized supermarket. By all appearances it was a clean, safe sanctuary located just outside of the less sanitized life of the inner city.

It was the neighborhood and era that produced the actor/governor Jesse Ventura. Most of the residents were blue-collar professionals who enjoyed spending time with their families, engaging in popular hobbies such as boating on the area's several lakes and rivers, and converting the family garage into a quaint sort of neighborhood recreation center, where the point of interest would be the care or restoration of some classic muscle car from the past. Within a mile was the cruising strip around the popular Lake Nokomis.

23

During the summer months, there would be an endless stream of seemingly carefree participants in their souped-up vehicles either making the scene or stealing the scene with their contribution to something only Americans understand, a spontaneous unsolicited parade-style tribute to Detroit.

Living two doors away from us was a typical family of five, a married couple with three kids: a daughter aged 20 and two boys, 17 and 15. The father was a career uniformed officer on the Minneapolis police force and owned a boat that he would dock in the summers a mile or two away on the Mississippi River. He would spend much of his free time on the boat and would allow his kids to use it with their friends in his absence. The boat was so large that when he brought it home in the fall, they had to remove a section of the wooden fence around their yard to store it next to their comparatively small house.

Families in America during the 1970s faced many similar challenges. There were generational issues between the young, newly self-liberated class of kids who felt entitled to blaze their own trails, suspicious of government and of those who wanted to restrict them in any way, while their parents held firm to the values and social structures that had brought them through the Great Depression, World War II, the Korean War, the Cuban missile crisis, and a national identity crisis. Looking back, I wonder what conflicts or pressures the oldest son faced as he was raised in a loving family, yet also in a greater environment that was very antipolice and antigovernment.

Unfortunately, we will never know why the oldest son shot himself that January. Maybe it didn't have much or anything to do with his environment. It could have been a problem with some other relationship or group of friends. Perhaps he didn't feel he could be successful at something that was extremely important to him. There was no note found, or any type of explanation. Nothing noticeably significant or revealing was happening in his world around that time. If you ask his father for reasons, he will tell you that not enough time or effort was put into the investigation, and that those in charge of the case were all too quick to assume the answers to some very large questions that the family had not even begin to consider. Were there unknown circumstances that would explain what happened? Were other people involved? Was it an accident? Perhaps it wasn't suicide. As in a huge percentage of situations like this, there is a bottomless question mark-shaped hole left in the hearts and minds of survivors, a hole that can be filled only with information given by someone who is no longer around.

Chapter 3

We Should've Seen It Coming

It seems universal that in tragic situations like this, clichés are tossed around: "We should've seen it coming" and "There's no way we could have known and there was nothing we could have done." I believe in today's world we can and must do better than that. I can tell you, the tools of understanding are available and the consequences for not using them are too great. I will clarify for you the constant thread that explains our human operating system. I will to show you that there is a simple set of patterns all people use to make sense of their world and take action from. In the upcoming chapters. I will map out the key points that really drive human behavior.

We see people who are doing the things that make them successful in terms of happiness, money, or some other sort of achievement, and we also see people at the opposite end of the scale, where their self-destructive behavior seems at odds with natural survival instincts. We think we understand why people want to be rich and successful (they want to be happy), and yet, only a few wealthy people consider themselves really successful. Many people are not succeeding in the areas they hold most important. Why not? It is not due to a lack of resources out there; many books have been written to assist us with personal and financial success. What about self-destructive behavior? Why do people intentionally do things destructive to themselves? Perhaps what is more important, how can we help them to see beyond their self-imposed limitations?

Looking at achievement this way, we can see a full range of natural behavior. I am suggesting that we can make sense of this full range in a way that empowers us to achieve our desired outcomes and consistently correct our course when dealing with adversity. In other words, this book sets out to make clear that we can see these things coming and there are things we can do, not only in extreme cases like suicide, but just as much in cases of hopelessness and feelings of isolation that kill the spirit as surely as any physical death. This knowledge empowers us to reach the goals that we all strive for easily navigating the invisible boundaries that most do not overcome. This book is not about suicide. It is about understanding people, including yourself, in a new way that you can use to give yourself and others a fulfilling life.

For me, changing self-destructive behavior is the true test of a strategy on how to live life. Unfortunately, like most of us, I have known several people who have committed suicide or who have wasted their lives with some form of self-destructive behavior such as severe drug addiction or gambling. I say the "true test" because I've always thought if you could understand why people do self-destructive things that they believe they have no control over, and deliver this understanding in a way that could help them change permanently, you would really serve people.

Clearly, this understanding of how to change self-destructive behavior needs to be a core strategy you can apply in real life. In real life we are confronted with challenges. They may be economic, they may involve our relationships with others and ourselves, and perhaps they are as individual as knowing our purpose in life. The same patterns that control destructive behavior also control the behavior and things we want more of in life. We want to be more successful in whatever area, but for some reason we find it difficult to consistently perform the actions that would strengthen our relationships, enable us to lose that extra weight, make a healthy income, and on and on. By understanding and changing our core strategy, our results will drastically improve, regardless of our environment.

This book is as real as your life. Where previous generalized information you've received may not have given you all the tools you need to make your life the way you want it, this book will. It will give you practical, strategy-level insights, useful no matter the size of your challenge or how high your goal. I need to set up with a few pages of essential background information and then we can quickly move into fun useful examples you can easily put to use in your daily life.

A natural response to tragic events where someone's life is wasted is to ask why it happened and what could have been done to prevent it. Many times, grief-stricken survivors act like detectives, frantically looking for clues that they hope will lead to understanding. For some survivors, it is to make sense of something that seems to makes no sense. For others it is to find meaning or just to gain closure. Perhaps even more for some, it is an understanding to enable return to a sense of predictability in their day-to-day lives. These everyday detectives look at the usual suspects, things like heredity, upbringing, abuse, or trauma. Did the person have things too hard . . . or too easy? Was the person's past or current situation so horrific that it is understandable that they would take their own life? Maybe the opposite was true: perhaps they did not appreciate how good they had it.

Answers to these normal questions help create a picture of an environment that may have contributed to these extreme behaviors, yet none of them is conclusive or satisfying in itself. We know that not all people with similar conditions or circumstances behave the same way. Although an understandable reaction, this sort of detective work usually falls short of creating certainties that help us understand this type of behavior, and it leaves us with no better answers than we had when we started. To understand extreme human behavior, really all human behavior, we need to have better reference points than those of environment and the stresses placed on the human nervous system. This book will reveal some very important and useful reference points in a way that will help you understand why we do the things we do while highlighting natural choices that serve us.

For me personally, having a drive for improvement, the important thing is the "aha" moment. Like the moment I noticed the core strategy that people were clinging to. That point when an understanding really hits home in a way that changes not only how we look at the world but also how we choose to act within it. An "aha" moment is when the way we make sense of things changes to a truer reflection of the world around us. It is as if a curtain were being drawn back to allow a clearer, more complete picture.

Chapter 4

So Why Don't We See It Coming?

To understand the view of suicides taking place in the 1970s and as late as the 1980s, Western psychology continued to improve, yet the stereotypes that were generally accepted in American society were still of the old school and off base: suicide and depression are mental illnesses and likely linked to heredity, or they indicate some weakness of character.

Currently, new psychiatric diagnoses are running the "flavor of the month," with tastefully coordinated designer drugs. According to current medical practice, control and coping seem to be the best outcomes one can hope for. I am not sure any drug claims to actually cure any of these "conditions." Managing the symptoms, as though the person's challenges were otherwise unavoidable, seems to be the accepted goal of modern medicine. In answering the question of whether that perspective is accurate or helpful, we may not be able to hold anyone accountable, especially when you consider that suicide is hard to predict and the cause of self-destructive behavior is a hard thing to diagnose.

Furthermore, not everyone who experiences depression, illness, or the loss of an important relationship commits suicide. When a suicidal person calls a suicide hotline, the counselor who answers the call will ask a series of questions designed to "assess risk." Studies have been conducted by major universities such as Columbia that confirm statistically that there are certain risk factors that can be identified, which, when present, increase the likelihood that the caller will take, or attempt to take, his or her life. In other words, this is one way to attempt to diagnose suicidal risk.

Here is a small sample of the questions recommended to identify risk factors:

- Has there been a recent tragedy?
- Has the person attempted suicide before?
- Is the person isolated from other people?
- Does the person have a plan and means to take their life?
- Has someone close to the person committed suicide?
- Is the person experiencing any of several types of psychological pain?
- Does the person believe they have options besides suicide?

The consensus among experts is that the more risk factors that stack up for a person, the greater the likelihood the person will make a suicide attempt. Research data supports the use of these important risk factors. It is the best information now given to the public and healthcare workers, but it is only a general picture and does not really predict suicide or provide a sufficient explanation of what is really going on as a cause. Many people who commit suicide never mention their plan to anyone or try to get help. Then too, there are people who can list several reasons to kill themselves and talk about it to everyone who will listen, but never do. So how can we understand in simple transparent terms what motivates people to enact such behavior, behavior that to them seems reasonable and rational?

To answer that question, a very brief and informal look at modern needs psychology and its basic origins is necessary to easily understand and tie together a true understanding of the ideas or strategies we introduce in this book.

Relax and have fun! There will not be a test. Remember too that the models discussed here are not complicated. They are really just very simple ideas or concepts like; *Needs, explain our behavior.*

Needs Models

For many years human behavior was thought to be motivated by the desire to satisfy various universal human needs. An early example of this type of theory was put forth by the Russian-born Serge Chakotin (1883–1973), student and successor of prominent Russian researcher Ivan Pavlov (1849–1936). (Pavlov himself is, of course, famous for his conditioned response research with dogs and a tuning fork.) Chakotin continued Pavlov's work in psychology and went on to author the 1940 classic, *The Rape of the Masses*. In that book he defined all human behavior as an attempt to satisfy four basic needs:

1. Struggle
2. Nutrition
3. Sexuality
4. Maternity

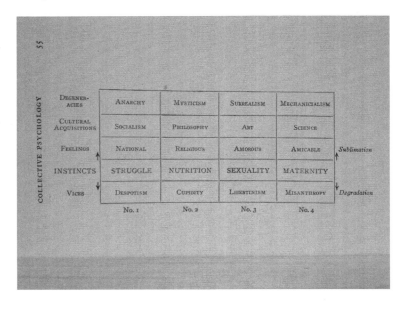

Figure 1.   Page 55 Rape of the masses.

Chakotin's Model of Human Needs.

The relevancy of Chakotin's ideas is perhaps in danger of being lost in translation from Russian and the context of a bygone era. Still his work remains hugely important because it reveals distinct relations between the tangible behaviors we see in people, driven by specific UN-tangible desires or needs we are all trying to satisfy.

Since then, other universal needs models have been built by many preeminent psychologists and used very successfully in understanding and redirecting unpleasant or unwanted human behavior. Likely the best recognized needs model in the United States is Abraham Maslow's (1908-1970) hierarchy of needs. Maslow whose parents were themselves Russian immigrants put forth his needs model in 1943 bearing a resemblance to Chakotin's work not only in need structure but also interpretation. Typically his model is illustrated in a pyramid shape. My understanding is that Maslow himself never used the pyramid, therefore I have reverted it to a grid form.

Physiological needs–breathing, eating, drinking, sleep, sex
Security needs–physical safety–freedom from attack
Social needs-interaction with people-belonging, affection, love
Psychological safety needs–self-esteem, reputation, status
Fulfillment and self-actualization needs

Figure 2. Maslow's Needs Model

First published in 1943

I was first introduced to Anthony Robbins' framework of needs in his "personal power" audio programs. In them he described all behavior as an attempt to satisfy the needs of

Love
Significance
Certainty
Uncertainty
Growth
Contribution

In the late 1980s or early 1990s, Robbins developed and began using human needs around these six words that seem to ring about as universally true as one could hope for. Using this six human needs framework, Robbins has done interventions at his wildly popular seminars that have changed unwanted human behaviors such as bad habits, "Stuckness," and so on into their opposites, with a speed and mastery that is the envy of a great many (if not all) trained psychologists who witness his work.

In 2002 he joined forces with internationally respected psychologist and family therapist Cloe Madanes, also an advanced practitioner in human needs psychology. Together they are promoting the use of needs and other psychology ideas, vigorously promoting education and awareness of their highly accepted and useful framework. They are perhaps psychology's most interesting odd couple in that her cutting-edge theory and application has made her a giant in the field of behavioral psychology compared to Tony, who is quick to project a comedic image as the king of the late-night infomercial, deliberately downplaying his competency and experience in rapid strategic intervention techniques. In real life Tony is a powerfully sculpted giant towering nearly 7 feet, while Cloe is a relatively small, attractive, sharply dressed, unassuming woman with a keen eye and a very feminine aura. Videos of their work can be found on Anthony Robbins's website.

All of these types of needs models share similarities to each other in the ideas of what specifically drives behavior. Other equally suitable words besides needs would be desire, emotional targets, drive, motivation, instincts, or even highly valued feelings.

It is also interesting that as we attempt to find one or two words that would have universal understanding for these drivers, when translated to English we find similar words. Ideas of struggle, security, physical safety, freedom from attack tend to translate in English to things like certainty, security, peace of mind, safety knowing that no catastrophe is imminent.

While survival is understood as the first law of nature, love is the one emotion that may rival its position in historic universal appeal and acceptance as a desired emotional target. As we look at Chakotin's chart, we see that he may have believed that love permeates different areas, or in translation he may be assigning it to amorous or amicable areas. Abraham Maslow has connected it with interaction with people, belonging, affection.

While Chakotin placed a marker (arrows) for higher and lower values for the needs; Vices to Instincts and Feelings to Cultural Acquisitions to Degeneracies, his distinctions between feelings and thoughts were not clearly defined, whereas Maslow did commit more strongly that certainty on a psychological level and the feelings of self-importance or significance of the intellectual level through self-esteem, reputation, status fulfillment and self-actualization are related. Of course the English words for those sorts of things would be self-importance, recognition from others, significance and so forth. Fulfillment and self-actualization could speak of personal growth and possibly contribution (similar to interaction with people, as in belonging). Meanwhile, Robbins has said the needs of growth and contribution are of a different class and refers to them as "needs of the spirit."

Two Other Non-Needs-Based Behavior Models

Other useful behavior models not based on needs have been developed and put to use over the years. One of the more popularized models is the Myers-Briggs Type Indicator. This behavior model is derived from the work of the Swiss-born psychoanalyst Carl Jung (1865–1961), who was a close associate of Sigmund Freud. Jung suggested the notion of personality types based on preferences for ways of psychological functioning. Isabel Myers (1897-1980) and her mother Katharine Briggs (1875-1968) developed a scale which measures where an individual falls on each of four of Jung's personality dimensions, yielding a composite score based on answers to a specific set of questions. Sixteen personality type combinations are possible, depending on the individual's scale positions. The slashes indicate one particular individual's scores. In this example, the individual is categorized as an INXT. (A scale score that is midway between the endpoints is coded as X.)

Introvert (I)----/--------------(E) Extrovert
Sensing (S)-----------/-------(N) Intuition
Judger   (J)---------/----------(P) Perceiver
Thinker (T)------/------------(F) Feeler

The Myers-Briggs distinctions have gone a long way to help average people to understand and work with the differences in people we all come across. For example, by understanding that someone else is more introverted than we are (has a higher score on the I-E scale than ours), we may cut them some slack and not insist that they be the life of the party or participate in activities that they are not comfortable with.

A common misconception in applying the Myers-Briggs model is that people always fall at one extreme or another. This is rarely the case. More helpful is to understand that each scale is a continuum and that most individuals have a tendency to fall either to the right or left of the midpoint in varying degrees. An informal reading can be obtained by rating an individual on each scale with a score of 1-10 based on a subjective assessment of the strength of that preference. Another common misconception is that Myers-Briggs scores are a fixed, permanent feature of an individual's identity. This is not the case. Scores can change over time and behaviors certainly change according to context and situation. Someone may be very outgoing and extroverted with their family, yet very tentative and introverted with strangers or new situations. Nevertheless, the Myers-Briggs Type Indicator has proved to be an excellent tool for understanding people and their behavior. We can identify what types of jobs people will like and how long they will likely stay at their job. Likewise, we can understand how to communicate better with others by learning how to speak in terms that they would appreciate. We can strengthen our relationships and close more sales with these tools.

It is important to note that self-destructive and self-empowering behavior occurs regardless of where anyone falls on any of these scales. No personality type leads to more self-empowering or more self-destructive behavior than any other. The Type Indicator is useful in helping us understand variations in behavior for the ways people deal with problems. Such as, a more introverted person may not feel as comfortable seeking help for a problem, and it is equally true that a more extroverted person can feel hopelessness due to not enjoying a deep relationship with anyone, despite having many friends and contacts.

The Myers-Briggs model is very popular, and a great number of people can tell you right off the bat what their own score is and have some knowledge of how to interpret the scores. Still, it can be very challenging to memorize and usefully apply all the nuances in tracking the impact of the model's various individual traits and combinations, and so very few people are really good at it.

Behavior models have become more complex since Chakotin. We like to think that the more complex and in depth they are, the better they are for understanding our complex behavior. Considering that premise, many say that one of the best models for understanding behavior was developed in the 1970s by Dr. Clare Graves

(1914-1986). After studying and teaching traditional psychology, he became frustrated by the incomplete understandings that were available. So he set out to formulate a theory that would predict and explain behavior in a practical sense. Mr. Graves passed away after completing his work and before it was popularized. Chris Cowan and Don Beck carried on with Graves's work and developed it into a working model that could be understood and taught. Graves's model took the form of a double helix. The work of Cowan and Beck is carried out under the name "Spiral Dynamics," and their model takes the form of a spiraling shell.

Spiral Dynamics works under several premises:

· Human behavior can be categorized to a definable evolutionary position.
· Human behavior evolves over time—it moves from a lower evolutionary position to a higher one.

The Spiral Dynamics model is credited with providing the understanding of human nature that ended apartheid in South Africa without bloodshed. Well, it is undoubtedly a valuable model. It is also very complex and requires extensive training to understand and apply its theories in a practical way.

All of these models or ideas help us to understand ourselves and each other better, but it is still apparent that we have a need to catch up in our ability to clearly and simply understand human mental-emotional processes. Our familiarity with the intricacies of these models can be likened to learning a foreign language, and most of us are perhaps at the level of a beginner, someone who is at the elementary stage of learning a new word for an everyday item. Let's say the word is toaster. In French it is *grille-pain* or *le toaster*. While the average person's understanding of complex psychological models is a good description for some things (we know what an introvert is), most of us are a long way from being fluent in a language based on any model, especially with no understanding of syntax, grammar, inferences, and the like. It is no wonder then that we can see someone in distress, even understand the problem, and yet have absolutely no idea what to do about it. The problem is, it's French. We may know how to say one or two words in French. That is just not enough. We can't help them, in the same way that we would have no idea how to go into a French department store and engage the sales associate to do a comparative analysis of the available toasters for sale, selecting the one that we know will suit our needs best.

Well, I have what I think is very good news. For most people, all the complex categorization and theory and training is not necessary. Going with our theoretical forebears, it may be that simple needs psychology, based on the idea that our behavior is driven by our unconscious desires to experience easily recognizable emotional states, is all we need for a useful and entirely practical understanding of any human behavior.

Do strategies explain Inner Conflict?

Most people would not argue with the presumption that the first law of nature is survival. This is likely what Chakotin's first human need referred to, the need he called "struggle." So why would someone operate in direct conflict with this most basic human need and take his or her own life? Does this mean there is another need that would or could intervene against what seems to be the most basic feature of human nature?

Unless a specific needs model can reveal needs conflicts, it may not help us diagnose or solve the most basic reasons people seek help to begin with: to understand and change unwanted behaviors, be they negative thinking, substance abuse, or self-sabotage—indeed, any behavior which is, on some level, self-destructive. Earlier I spoke of suicide, mainly because it is perhaps the most extreme example of conflicted or self-destructive behavior. But frankly, inner conflict is the important issue: Exactly why do people take any action that is self-destructive in some way?

Also, why do people repeatedly fail to do the things that they know are good for themselves?

So many lives are flushed away and opportunities lost as a result of negative behavior, and this includes the abuse of drugs, alcohol, and cigarettes. Countless people are affected negatively by patterns of family violence, hopelessness, and poverty, even though they live in an environment that is capable of sustaining more positive results. Consciously we know that smoking and excessive drinking are bad for us, and we know the importance of healthy eating. So why do we continue to do unhealthy things in spite of our knowledge and true desire to change?

Could it be that these kinds of destructive behaviors are not determined by conscious decisions, that these choices to harm ourselves are not made based on our best knowledge, but on something else? What is going on? What is the "something else"? Is there a definable decision point occurring outside of awareness that determines what we will ultimately do?

To me, the answer is clearly *yes*.

Does awareness of these hidden processes and inner conflicts give us the ability to make choices in those areas in a way we never could before? Again, I believe the answer is yes, and that any understanding has to be basic enough for us to use, and thorough enough to have an impact. Not that understanding alone is always 100% of the solution. I believe someone must also possess a strong desire for change. Without a desire strong enough to motivate us to take action for a clear outcome, the behavior now taking place may be considered good enough. With that in mind, let's simplify things and speak in English so that we can understand and apply solutions to inner conflict right away with ourselves and others.

Strategies as a Key to Understanding.

The framework for strategies is unique in that it is a marked departure from basic needs models. The strategy is best understood as a key, and our needs are like the tumblers of a lock lining up on the key. Only a key cut and positioned correctly relative to the tumblers will open the lock and obtain our desired result.

A properly shaped strategy easily aligns and satisfies our unconscious needs.

Strategies is about understanding how and why our keys are cut so that we can recut them to break lifelong limiting patterns.

When you look at a typical house key. You will notice that most keys have a straight edge and a jagged edge on the end that is inserted into the lock. The straight edge and the grooves running front to back on the key serve as guides to fit the key in its proper place. The important part, the part that makes this unique, is the jagged edge or the way it is cut. It is cut in a fashion to align a set of tumblers within the lock to the edge of the little circle that has the keyhole, allowing the key to turn and work as a lever to pull the bolt back.

In this example I'm saying that the notches in the key, or the way it's cut, represents our belief of how we need to be to operate in the world and successfully satisfy our emotional desires. In other words, lining up and opening the lock of happiness in life.

Until we consciously cut our keys, they will not be properly fitted for our highest ideals and standards as humans. Rather, they will be set to our primal standards based more on survival, self-centeredness, and conditioning. This is because historically mankind's behavior is shaped (like the key) from an early age based on our interaction with the world in a variety of situations. Historically, this shaping of our behavior has taken place since before our use of language and possibly even before what we now know to be conscious awareness. The abilities we are born with to take care of ourselves and survive are not dependent on our conscious awareness of them. In other words, you won't die if you don't understand this process; however, your ability to reach certain desired emotional targets will be much more restricted.

As a species, we naturally adjust our behavior to our environments without the necessity of thinking about it. When those adjustments are made at an early age or otherwise out of consciousness, they are made at our strategy level. They're made from a place before thought and emotion are internalized as different things. That is to say, where both emotions and thoughts are harmonious, natural contributors to our decision process.

When our actions and reactions to the environment are unconsciously accepted as appropriate through repetition or intensity, we become in a sense like Pavlov's dogs, automatically reacting to unconscious directives of behavior.

When the dogs salivate excessively at the introduction of the sound of the tuning fork, we have no problem recognizing their mistake. In this way we see the importance of context and circumstance. Even though our lives are possibly more attuned to social interaction and circumstance than physical circumstance, we make the same kinds of mistakes as the dogs.

We are conditioned through our experience how to react when presented with both social and physical situations. If we are insulted, we will have a response that we believe is appropriate. There's a large range of responses determined by how someone's key is cut. While one person may wish to lash out physically, another may believe it appropriate to respond with a more severe insult. Another person may believe it inappropriate to interact on such a level and refuse to participate. This is how the key is cut that represents their strategy level decisions. They will probably conclude that their response is of good judgment and others should come around to their way of thinking on the matter.

Even though our key was cut somewhat outside of our awareness, we trust that it is correct, and we tend to believe that we are shaped correctly to reach our emotional targets; therefore we believe any problems are due to something external such as circumstance.

Because of this we start to look, not at how we believe we should behave in our environment to feel fulfilled, but rather, we believe we need to change our environment to become fulfilled. Therefore we seek ways to fill up emotionally by having more things, blaming people for our circumstance, or trying to change others, so that we will feel better.

This is easy to see in others, of course, like when people move from relationship to relationship experiencing the same type of problems in each. They blame their partner or circumstances as they keep trying, like a key trying to find the lock that will open for them. People even tell them, "Look, this is an issue with you that you must resolve or you will have the same problem in your next relationship." Even if they understand and agree with the truth in that thinking, they may not know how to resolve or change themselves.

One more fun quick example of a core strategy can be found in the current movie "Alice in Wonderland" where the Red Queen continually reaffirms her obviously wrong choice in answering the question "is it better to be loved or feared?" She affirms it is better to be feared and behaves like a tyrant, yet her sadness at the impact of that behavior is apparent. We can begin to notice that her internal conflict stems from her stern core strategies failure to fulfill her needs. While her top desire is for love and meaningful connection with others she is stuck using her strategy of self-importance, domination and control.

The Key-maker, Sounding-boards

Understanding how these strategy keys are naturally cut gives us the ability to understand ourselves and change things we do not like relating to what we do and how we feel. This is a little detailed, but it is well worth following along.

First let's introduce a new term that you'll need to understand. The term is "sounding board." I use this term because we are familiar with the idea of bouncing an idea off of a sounding board. Even though we are familiar with the term, most of us have not really given it a great deal of thought. For our purposes here we will consider some deeper implications of a sounding board. People usually think of sounding boards as simple and flat, giving a true answer to whatever idea is being bounced off of them. In my way of using sounding boards, I believe they are rarely a reflection of the impartial evaluative judgment we are seeking. I believe they are a multitude of randomly organized ideas presented as grounds for valid consideration based more on the original emotional intensity than anything else. These "sounding boards," as I call them, I believe demonstrate how we operate on an emotional language before learning a verbal language. They are conditioned responses (like reflexes) meant to ensure our physical and emotional survival.

Let's consider a circumstance where someone very young nearly falls from a great height to their death. From that point on they may have a very strong fear of heights, perhaps at a ridiculous level. Or, for a funny example, Frankenstein who would only repeat two words, "Fire bad," implying his recollection of a negative experience with the villagers who wished to burn him

If we think about these examples, they show something very helpful. They show that when the person is evaluating something involving an emotionally charged previous experience, the recollection of the experience becomes a sounding board in their evaluation process. This occurs no matter how unwarranted the fear is in the current circumstance. This is true whether it is a fear of physical things like insects, animals, heights, or purely emotions or thoughts such as love, boredom, frustration, and such. So we can predict that if we were to ask Frankenstein to sit by the camp fire, he would reference his internal sounding board, become terrified, and decline the offer, no matter how dearly he loves S'mores or our good company.

Think about it, people constantly talk about previous experience as excuses for future behavior. One of the most frequently used excuses for not fully committing to an intimate relationship is that something did not go right in the last relationship. Think of something you really like to do and something else that you used to like to do and there is no way you would do it now. In each case notice the sounding board you produce that reinforces your decision.

These sounding boards are what shape our core strategy key. They can cut a groove in our key in one fell swoop with a highly charged emotional event, or they can slowly cut a groove through repetition, either intentionally or not.

By understanding this process we can reshape our strategy key to fit any lock we desire.

If you ever felt frustrated, like you didn't understand the rules of life, or how to play the game of life, much less how to win at it, get excited, because that is changing now.

Chapter 5

Like the Strings of a Puppet

Strategy--Demystifying and Unlocking the Unconscious

The Austrian Sigmund Freud (1856–1921), one of our best known and most influential Psychiatrists, came up with or at least popularized the idea of the unconscious mind, a concept which had been floating around since the 1800s. This idea has been a blessing and a curse for many. It is a blessing in that it recognizes the need to more clearly define mental processes that occur outside of our awareness. It is a curse in that it can imply that there is part of us we will never understand because, by definition, we cannot be conscious of it. Therefore, we could never understand it or fully control ourselves. In other words, it is a paradox. Just thinking about the unconscious is difficult.

As the Polish philosopher (among other things) Alfred Korzybski (1879-1950) pointed out in his landmark 1933 book, *Science and Sanity*, the book that started the discipline of general semantics, "Unconscious is an undefined term, as it lacks content." Or, as we might ask, unconscious of what? Studying and trying to describe a part of the psyche as a dark murky place, full of things that are unknowable, does not provide instruction for what to do about it. This enterprise seems more advantageous for the psychoanalyst in the lengthy and expensive task of interpretation. Therefore, when I use the term "unconscious" in this book, I am not talking about a certain part of someone's body. I use the term only to differentiate events that occur outside of an individual's awareness from those that do occur with awareness.

So, for our purposes, what is it exactly that we should be conscious of, and how will that help us? First, it's helpful to be conscious of how these needs I've mentioned affect our feelings and actions. Most of us are familiar with the phrase "having your buttons pushed." It refers to someone coming along and doing something that causes a person to have an emotional reaction, usually without that person's consent. It's interesting, though, that an action that gets a certain reaction from one person may not work in the same degree for another, or maybe not at all. The reaction is not automatic; it is an illumination of an inner process unique to the person having the reaction.

It would be helpful if we understood the nature of the inner process that is being illuminated. Meaning, all of us have similar "buttons," and there is an understandable dynamic behind all the different reactions. Going back to look at basic human needs in the manner laid out by Chakotin and his successors, we will see shortly many ways in which everyone's buttons and reactions work.

Chapter 6

Button Pushers

As mentioned earlier, a need is an emotional desire that will likely motivate us to action. We can use the buttons analogy in a slightly different way, turning it around to talk about when something wanted or positive happens when these buttons are pushed instead of something angry or anxious. Our needs could be likened to powerful forces that live behind nine buttons that we all have and feel very compelled to have pushed. Needs, then, for our purposes, can be described as "emotional targets." They represent the feelings and states that we perceive unconsciously as rewards for our actions. They are what motivates us. Pushing our buttons in this good sense may make us feel loved, important, validated, certain.

The reasons that we do things, or have a desire for something specific, can be traced back to a feeling we have about the thing desired. Think for a moment about anything that you want in your life, and notice there is a feeling you expect to experience when you get it. In some cases we take action because we are afraid of the bad feeling we will experience if we fail to take action. In either case, we are motivated to do something by the expectation of a feeling. That feeling can be called an "emotional target." The desired emotional targets can be simplified into specific categories, so that we can understand them more easily.

Much human behavior can be understood by understanding an individual's emotional targets. The motivation for someone to tell a joke to a group of friends, for example, can be traced back to specific needs that person is trying to satisfy. Different people might tell the same joke to the same people, but in doing so, each may be trying to satisfy very different personal needs. One may tell the joke to feel connection with others, another person may tell the joke to feel important, and another to bring variety to the situation.

By bringing need-based processes into consciousness and having a model like the one you're learning, you will understand your own behavior and that of others in a much more self-empowering way. When needs operate outside of consciousness, as targets we wish to hit, we may feel inner urges to do things that are contrary to our own values and beliefs of how we should be. So, as we are trying to hit these targets. They are in turn directing the course of our lives, and we are not even aware of it! All we know is that our life either is, or is not, going the direction we would like.

It is vital that we become aware of our emotional targets. With awareness of the targets, we can harmonize with our unconscious processes and satisfy our most basic and important human needs, and do so in ways that we have consciously chosen—ways that feel good, are good for others, and serve the greater good. This awareness leads to an achievable and sustainable state of fulfillment.

Chapter 7

Introducing the Strategy Framework

Needs are emotional targets. For simplicity, each need is represented by a single word. Words by themselves can, of course, have several different meanings. I will be using these words in very specific ways, and their meaning for us will be determined by the context in which we will be using them. In the time since the idea of needs was first proposed, different words with different levels of importance were put together as models. As time goes by these models continue to become increasingly refined and effective in therapy or change work.

I will be talking about needs like love; however, I will not be using Chakotin, Maslow, or Robbins definitions. In other words, Tony Robbins has a specific way that he speaks about love, certainty, and other needs. Those particular uses and definitions will not be used here unless specified.

The unique framework for this book is in support of the idea that understanding the idea that "Core Strategy" reduces resistance to conscious change, helping the person align themselves with their own desires. Therefore the framework is that "Core Strategy" is a *master need* and there are universal emotional drivers of validation, love, self-worth, purpose, and so on. Their importance is based, not on a pre-established hierarchy, but rather importance is determined on how highly each individual values them.

The 6 Human Needs, is a concept developed and popularized by Tony Robbins. I have taken the liberty to add to it in this book according to my own thinking. I fully love and support Tony's six needs model and am in no way suggesting that it or any other model lacks anything. I am saying, Strategies" is a unique concept that can only be understood relative to our universal emotional drivers. With that clarified, I would say that although they are totally different ideas and frameworks, they do complement each other very well, and I encourage anyone interested to familiarize themselves with the work of Robbins, Maslow, and Chakotin. Any coincidences in the definitions or their uses will likely be of a thematic or "generally accepted" nature because we must remember that no matter who developed any particular framework, the outcome for its use has always been the same.

Let me introduce my definitions of these drivers relative to the true marrow of our being - our core strategy level.

Let's get started . . .

*Note: Headers show one way to group the various models based on a general description.

Need One: Certainty, Struggle, Survival

Certainty may be synonymous with struggle as presented in the earliest Russian model. It also represents what we know as the will to live.

Historically, many martial systems have placed high value on acting on this emotional driver. For many, survival is understood as the first law of nature. When a person is placed in a life or death situation, unless the person is otherwise trained or conditioned, the metaphoric survival button has been pushed, providing motivation that we can understand that will lead to the person taking action. Because this reflex is generally so well understood by people, I'm using it as our first example. It is also a good depiction of how the other needs also serve us and how they are triggered automatically.

This reaction can easily be understood at a primal or instinctual feeling level.

This need for certainty also turns up on a more intellectual or thinking level in the way we reason. Intellectually our thoughts require a foundation or a premise of certainty to which we can attach our plans or ideas. Without premises of certainty, it is like trying to hang a picture in midair.

Let me explain. We need points of reference from which to operate. For example, we need to act as if the sun will come up tomorrow, or that we will see each other again, (even though these things may not actually happen or even be objectively true). Without the ability to place some intellectual certainty on the likelihood of future events, our brains would quickly become overwhelmed with all the possible ways the future could unfold. Operating with that intellectual certainty allows us to act as though our generalizations and predictions about the future will be true.

I hope I have clarified the distinctions between certainty at the thinking and feeling levels. If not, it's okay, we will make it clearer it with more examples as we go. Within those two levels the need for certainty can motivate us in several ways.

The need for certainty may motivate us . . .

- To properly care of ourselves so that we do not become decrepit.
- To stay in a job we hate just to have the certainty of a roof over our head.
- To stay in a bad relationship because at least we know what we have and are certain we are in control.
- To be conservative in how we plan our lives.

To sum up, the need for certainty can be seen as a motivator for planning and action (positive or negative) that usually reflects an avoidance of uncertainty. Consider someone with large family obligations and long-term debt who learns that his job may be eliminated. The need to recover certainty may preoccupy his attention to an extreme degree.

Someone attempting to satiate the need for certainty may even act in otherwise uncharacteristic ways. For instance, a normally withdrawn or introverted person may demand that the boss or others provide clarity in situations of possible negative consequence, such as terms of employment, relationships, benefits, and remuneration. The person may be so preoccupied with the need for certainty in clarifying an employer's exact commitment that he may be impaired in his ability to make a reasonable contribution to his job duties. This drive for certainty in a work context may damage relationships or at least raise eyebrows about the appropriateness and judgment of the employee. Yet the person may not be able to stop themselves. Of course, if an employer comes to understand that this behavior is motivated by the need for certainty, and learns how to meet that need, the result may be that the employee will come to intensely protect the relationship, including the employer's interests, to everyone's advantage.

Webster's says needs are "a physiological or psychological requirement for the well-being of an organism." They are called needs because they are requirements. They are not optional. Everyone must regularly satisfy the need for the feeling of certainty. However, different individuals do have different opinions for what it will take to feel certain, and we have different levels of emotional intensity relating to how we strive for certainty. Someone with an intense emotional desire for certainty will behave drastically differently from someone with a more so-so attitude toward certainty.

A good example would be a person who grew up in poverty and is motivated to do whatever it takes to make sure that he never experiences the uncertainty of poverty again. Contrast that with a person who grew up in a resource or certainty-rich environment and becomes lazy or restless due to a surfeit of security.

Need Two: Variety, Movement, Anarchy, Difference

We also truly need uncertainty, or we could call it variety, the experience of difference and novelty. Just think about it: Our whole system of perception operates on the principle of difference. We can only talk about things in terms of how they are alike and or how they are different, because, other than in our imagination, in reality, no two things are exactly identical. In some cases, the differences could be small or not even perceivable, and yet there are always differences in location, time, and usage. At the tiniest microscopic levels, the differences in two or more similar items are more apparent. Our nervous systems and our five senses are geared to receive what some NLP practitioners call "news of difference." It is by these differences that we make distinctions about our environment, allowing us to function within it.

Imagine a world where there is only one visual image to see, only one sound to be heard, only one surface texture to be felt, one taste, and one smell, and each of those things are permanent. Such an environment would quickly drive us to madness. All of our senses are designed to distinguish and relay the differences in our environment. Physically we need an environment where we can make distinctions. Like the need for certainty, the need for variety operates on an intellectual level as well as on a primal emotional feelings level. Many studies on intellectual variety have shown that degenerative mental conditions can be prevented by keeping the mind active through tasks which challenge the mind with variety, by demanding creativity. Working the mind, just as with a muscle, it seems, has the effect of developing strength and endurance. Novelty, variety, or challenge is positive stimulation that gives the mind a good workout in creating new internalizations of things in our environment, whether real or imagined.

The level of drive or importance of the need for variety may change over a person's life. Younger people may value variety much more than certainty, and as they get older they may tend to shift and value certainty over variety. Sometimes a life change can cause someone to value certainty more than variety, such as the addition of a child, the death of a loved one, or the end of some highly valued long-term commitment.

Need Three: Significance, Self Esteem, Reputation, Status

The third need, the need for the feeling of significance, importance, or uniqueness, is possibly the easiest need to spot and the toughest to discuss with someone. We all have a need to feel that our lives are relevant, that we matter, that we make a difference. We see it in kids who want attention and want to be noticed. They don't just want to feel important, they need to feel important in a way that distinguishes them from others or their siblings—so much so that if one child behaves strongly in a specific way that gets attention, often another child may act in the opposite way just to be distinguished and get attention. If one child is "the good child," another child may be "the bad child." Being the bad child may get them more attention and more significance then the good child. What we should notice here is that the behavior is satisfying the need for significance.

We see it in teenagers who compete to stand out in some way (without, of course, being *so* different that they lose the admiration of their peers). We see it in adults who try to project an image of accomplishment or taste. Luxury car sales worldwide are fueled by and serve the need for significance. Every one of us operates as though we have at least one unique property—skill or knowledge or connection—that makes us significant. When you positively acknowledge someone's way of satisfying their need for significance, you will likely make an ally of them. These properties of significance are many and various: your uncle's interesting ability to memorize the history of postage stamps, or your blank in-law's fascinating memorabilia collection, or so-and-so's ability to eat or drink enough of some unhealthy substance that would normally kill a horse.

Some of humankind's greatest achievements, as well as most embarrassing moments, have been a result of someone trying to satisfy the need for significance. Everyone must regularly satisfy all of their needs, including the need for significance. Significance, however, is the one that most people feel uncomfortable with. Some people refuse to acknowledge they are satisfying this need in spite of behavior that may seem otherwise. Even humble people may practice humility at a level that yields significance.

No one has to feel uncomfortable. It is fine to satisfy your need for self-esteem. We all must. The thing to keep in mind is the *way* in which we satisfy that need. We have choices. We can satisfy the need in ways that are good for ourselves, are good for others, and serve the greater good. Or we can satisfy that need in ways that are not good for us, not good for others, and do not serve the greater good. When we empower ourselves to satisfy our need for significance based on what is good for everyone involved, our relationships with ourselves, others, and our environment will be much stronger and more positive.

Need four: Love and Connection

The emotion of love has been a favorite topic since humanity started recording and sharing information. It has always been one of the principal themes with which theater, art, history, and philosophy weave together meaningful content that resonates with us all. It is said to be the strongest of the emotions. We all have some direct experience of love with people, animals, nature, God, or life. We all know that love is powerful in motivating us to do interesting or extreme things. Strong bonds are created when the emotion of love is shared between people, or even between a person and a beloved pet. The loss of the shared loving connection can affect us on a level like no other loss.

This need is rooted in some very solid facts. People do not live in isolation. We are interdependent and rely on each other for survival on both physical and emotional levels. Even in antisocial people, the opinions of others matter. Antisocial people typically have strong emotions regarding how they would like to have an impact on and be perceived by others. Even suicidal bombers and gunmen often leave manifestoes or written documentation describing their dismay that a more utopian civilization does not exist, and that their act was a product of how they needed to respond to this imperfect environment. Even in these rare extreme negative cases, the need for connection is clearly driving the behavior.

More compelling evidence that love is a need and not merely a desire comes from the discovery by doctors in orphanages who learned that babies who were left alone and not loved and held would die. How can this be so? Is this not solid proof that there is a connection between our emotional state and our physical well-being? Many studies continue to verify associations like these. One fairly well-known example is the work of Dr. John Gottman, a researcher and marital therapist with the University of Washington who has gathered years of data showing a definite connection between negative emotions in intimate relationships and increased health risks for the partner receiving the negative emotion. The most negative of the emotions, according to his research, is contempt. According to Gottman, contempt is the most toxic to a relationship because it rejects the person at the level of identity. To have someone you care about exhibit contempt to you is not only emotionally damaging, but also has measurable negative effects your health.

Need five: Self Actualization, Growth, Fulfillment

Throughout humanity's history and everywhere in the world can be found themes of expansion/contraction, Yin and Yang, advance and retreat. The underlying idea here is that nothing is static. Even as you read this, your body in this world is in a state of flux, in a process of change at subatomic levels, never to be repeated. Nothing is ever completely inactive; it is either increasing or decreasing, growing or dying. Like the old saying says, "Use it or lose it." When we stop using or fail to use our resources, apathy can set in—and things can really start going downhill! To reverse this, we must reignite the process of growth.

Rate yourself 1-10 in these categories of your life. Are you growing or dying?

- Your intimate relationship
- Your career
- Your health
- Your personal development
- Your relationship with friends and family

· Your spiritual relationship

In the categories where you gave yourself high numbers, you probably experience good feelings regularly. The others? Well, pay attention to them! They will have an impact on your overall state, because you're likely neglecting them.

Need six: Contribution, Cultural Acquisitions

We do not live in isolation. On some level we have a relationship with every other person on the planet, and that relationship is based on how we think and feel about specific people we know, as well as groups of anonymous strangers. The relationship between you and everyone you perceive is based primarily on your own definition of that relationship. As Cassius Keyser (1862-1947) said, "To be" is "to be related." It is by the relationships and outcomes we define with others and our environment that we come to understand our own identity and purpose.

Is your relationship with the greater world defined by scarcity or by abundance? Do you worry about resources, or are you confident that there is plenty for everyone? How about others? Do they take from you or do they add value to your life by their presence?

Just as growth speaks of living and dying, contribution speaks of adding something or draining something. By contributing to others and your environment, you come to shape your own self-view and opinion of your own resources in a positive, hopeful way. You begin to realize that not only do you have enough to take care of yourself, you have additional resources to contribute to others and possibly the greater good. You are acknowledging your own resources, and by linking yourself—what you're doing and the outcomes of what you do—as much with the needs of others as your own, you will be in harmony with yourself and your environment in a very fulfilling way.

Here's a vital clue about how important contribution is, as pointed out by Tony Robbins: Excess focus on self and feelings of personal impoverishment are always present in cases of depression.

Need Seven: Validation

One of the strongest needs we have is the need for validation or affirmation, also seen as the need to be right, or to be accepted and appreciated just as we are. It's no wonder, either. Think about it. We evaluate situations and take countless thousands of actions every day, at all levels of significance, from large-scale life decisions, to decisions about our identity, to the moment-to-moment decisions we make all day long about mundane matters such as what kind of toothpaste to buy. All of these actions are based on information we have carefully collected and evaluated throughout our lives.

Each time we take an action, it alters the course of our life, a little or a lot, for ourselves and others. Imagine how difficult life would be if you felt anxious and unsure every time you did something! We all like to think that we know what we are doing and talking about most of the time, and that we have a handle on life's challenges (or at least can come up with one pretty quickly).

To live life successfully, we need to be good evaluators. We live our lives based around the assumption that we have collected enough good information to enable us to survive—to evaluate situations facing us well enough to enable us to make the right decisions. Validation is when we get feedback telling us that our evaluative process is working correctly (whether it is or not). Unconsciously we are attempting to satisfy this need for validation and confirm our abilities constantly.

This is an extremely powerful need. We need to believe that our perspective is accurate, that we know what we are doing, and that all the information we have evaluated up to this moment has led us to the good conclusions that we now logically and emotionally operate from. It's very painful to doubt ourselves in this. (To make things even worse, when we doubt our ability to evaluate, it can make us dysfunctional evaluators.) We like to be *right*. Validation allows us to experience a sense of being good enough.

We tend to enjoy the company of people with views and beliefs similar to our own because they boost our confidence in our evaluation ability—they validate us. We also like the company of people who would like to be like us. They give us compliments and validate us by appreciating our way of evaluating and being.

The opposite of validation is devalidation, which is what happens when you tell someone their evaluative process is wrong. That's all it is. But in real life, being invalidated is for many people a kind of torment and suffering. In real life, we don't usually say to John, "Hey, John, your evaluative process is wrong." We might mean that, but we are much more likely to say, "Hey, John, *you're* wrong." This is subtly yet entirely different, because this is a statement that hits John on the level of his identity. John is very likely to hear you making him wrong *as a person*. The devalidation hits him on a level he cannot defend. He <u>can</u> change how he evaluates, that's one thing, but he <u>cannot</u> change himself at the level of identity quite so easily. Devalidation usually feels like a very personal attack on a person's core strategy. Tony Robbins promotes the idea that the greatest universal human fear is that, if we are not enough, we will not be loved, or we will be rejected or ignored. So, in practice anyway, validation can be understood as an opposite of rejection; acceptance at the level of a person's core strategy.

Let's take the common fear of public speaking as an illustration of how great the need for validation is. Most Americans are probably familiar with the popular survey that showed that the number one greatest fear of an unexpectedly large majority was public speaking, that is, standing in front of a large group of people and making a verbal presentation. Even more shocking was that some people expressed a greater fear of public speaking than of their own death. When we understand the need for validation, this makes perfect sense. When you're standing up in front of a large group of people, you will be judged. Somebody might think you are wrong. That's a great deal of pressure, and not entirely unfounded. People do tend to form opinions about public speakers that may not be so easily changed. This fear works in a vicious cycle: If you're nervous, you're even more likely to make a mess of yourself. Many of us avoid this occasion for massive devaluation by never speaking up at all.

In my own experience working with thousands of people worldwide, I have yet to find an instance where Tony's generalization doesn't fit: When people believe they are seen as a poor evaluator/decision-maker, or wrong, or "not enough" in some way, they fear that they will be rejected, ignored, or unloved.

For many, failing in something (even if we have tried hard) equals or means failure as a person, and that equals or means becoming undeserving of love. Definitely a lose/lose equation. So when we validate someone, even for something relatively insignificant, we are helping them move their focus from a fear greater than death and into confident self-acceptance.

Need Eight: A Goal, Outcome, or Purpose

Reasoning is impossible without a goal or outcome.

This is important, so I will repeat it.

Reasoning is impossible without a goal or outcome.

Think about that for a moment.

Decision-making and evaluating is the process of asking and answering internal questions. You can ask yourself if that last statement is true and realize that, of course, it is. The only way you can judge the answer to your internal question-answer session is to see how the answer relates to your outcome. When you asked yourself if the first sentence in this paragraph was true or not, your goal was to determine the truth. Without that goal, you would not get the answer. If instead your goal had been to determine how many words were in the statement, the answer would be quite different. The answer would be 12.

This exercise illustrates how thoughts do not require goals, but reasoning does.

Many of our goals are unconscious. We have thousands of habitual goals that operate to direct our behavior and actions without our even needing to bring them to conscious awareness. We don't have to think about getting out of bed or eating breakfast, or showering, yet all these actions work to serve our larger goals such as getting to work, school, or just down to the park. When we have an important goal, such as maintaining our employment, our unconscious usually handles the process of evaluating if the actions we are taking are in line with our goals or not. It dutifully alerts us when we move too far away from that goal. The unconscious is also where we store what I like to call generalized sounding boards, such as "doing the right thing." When you ask yourself a question like "Should I wear this plaid shirt?" it provides a sounding board for your actions and gives you an immediate answer you can use, such as, "No, that shirt would definitely make the boss think I am strange/not executive material."

Concrete, conscious goals like running a triathlon or making a million dollars give us great sounding boards for the evaluative process to function. The point is, without a goal, any evaluation process is merely meaningless, random thought falling short of productive reasoning. This clearly explains why so many people with no coherent goal or desired outcome, or several contradictory outcomes, can endlessly mull over questions and answers about how to continue and yet produce ambiguous and unsatisfactory results.

I call *goals* a need because all decisions and action we take are based relative to something we want to have or avoid. By recognizing directly how incredibly influential goals are, not only for thought but also for the emotional quality of our lives, we can give them the important attention they require. After all, what is the difference in the emotional quality of someone's life whose goal in the family is to *survive and not be taken advantage of* versus another's, whose goal is to *be an outstanding contributor and role model reinforcing the idea that there is joy and purpose in life?*

Need Nine: A Strategy

The book is titled after this need, because we all need one. We all need an unconscious methodology we believe will best satisfy all our needs, given our perceptions about ourselves and our environment. That's a mouthful, but what does it mean? It means on some level *everyone believes they are doing the best they can to satisfy their needs with the resources they have.* They realize they might be able to do it even better if they had more help or knowledge, or whatever, but for now, they are doing exactly as much as they are able to do. Strategy includes our sense of ourselves that we endorse and present to others.

It is the determiner of what we feel is appropriate for ourselves (and others) to be, do, and have, throughout our lives.

It is a thread of conviction that runs in the same way through the captain of a whaling ship and his adversary, the captain of a Greenpeace ship. It is the profound sense in each of us about how we need to be to satisfy our most valued needs.

Strategy provides ways to satisfy our need to feel as though what we are doing is right. As in, right for us.

Our strategy leads us to do things that are unique and that define us. As an example, we may want to be seen as kind, good-humored, or smart because our experiences have led us to conclude that it is beneficial (need-satisfying) to be seen that way, and we therefore take on behavior that matches this belief. Our evaluative process has selected the best way for us to function in our environment to meet our needs. Once we have resolved with ourselves that our behavior is appropriate, we no longer feel a need to evaluate it, and it becomes an unconscious process. Note this down for later: We do this regardless of whether the behavior currently serves us.

Everyone is running their strategy. Everyone, all the time, and they are usually proud of it. In a way, strategy is what gets us through life. When you see someone in a lifestyle you find strange or doing something that you do not understand, you need to know that that person nevertheless believes that what he or she is doing is an excellent strategy.

The guy with 10,000 tattoos? That is part of his strategy. He likely satisfies most or all of his needs at high levels through his appearance.

He will get a reaction—that is certain.
He knows he will have variety from the different reactions he will get.
He knows he will get love: a hot tattooed honey or at least connection from his tattoo-wearing peer group.
He knows he is significant, because not too many people are willing to be that extreme.
He knows he will grow because he is working on his unique persona.
He knows he will contribute by validating a growing peer group.
He knows many will validate his artwork. If not, he can run a sub-strategy of prejudgment of them and feel even better about himself.
Certainly he has a goal relating to his tattoos—a number, a body percentage, a theme.

Let's look at somebody who would seem to be that guy's opposite: a middle-aged Avon lady. She's running a strategy too.

She knows she will get maximum good vibes from others by being very neat, clean, and proper—certainty and connection.
She gets significance by holding herself to a standard that others do not.
She gets variety by changing her look with the seasons and holidays.
She feels validated being similar to beautiful, successful-appearing people in magazines, and certainly the salespeople selling her all that stuff give her plenty of validation.
She contributes by setting an example.
She may feel growth by staying on top of the latest trends.
We can lightheartedly surmise that her goal is median-plus income, 2.5 children, a lovely suburban home with double garage, and the perfect husband.

Chapter 8

Unlocking the Needs

Why do I give these generalized examples of need-satisfying strategies? We've briefly described what human needs are, but so what? Why is it important to talk about them?

It is important because, as it turns out, our understanding of human needs gives us a unique perspective on human behavior. This helps us to reshape our key. Although human needs are relatively simple and easy to understand, the deep and far-reaching consequences of their application are extraordinary.

Human needs are the invisible targets behind all the actions that you and I make during our lives. When we understand them, we can take charge of our strategies and aim directly at the now-visible target. That means we can clearly pinpoint various kinds of emotional fulfillment quickly and easily, and what is more, win them! Without this knowledge, we might not even be quite sure what it is we are after.

When most people are asked what they want in life, they cannot tell you exactly what that is. Still they know they want *something*. If you press them for an answer, they will usually say they want *more* of something: I want more money, time, joy, love. A universal problem with those type of answers is that, if you give them more money, time, joy, love, they will be happy for a little while, but soon they will be back to experiencing a feeling of lack in the area they said they desired most. On the other hand, if you understand the real needs that are driving you at an unconscious level, you'll be able to unlock your own inner sense of fulfillment for the long-term.

This knowledge won't be limited to just you: You will be able to understand and help others in a way you may not have believed possible. We are involved in and responsible for so many interpersonal relationships throughout our lives. One of the most challenging relationships can be our intimate relationship with our spouse or partner. With so many marriages ending in divorce, it is fair to say that the skill of understanding ourselves and others in the context of a relationship is long overdue.

When you understand your partner's need structure (the order and value they place on each need) you are then empowered to re-cut your key to better match his or her needs and bring your relationship to a new level of success. Most people are frustrated in their relationship. Many of us give up because we no longer feel we can make our partner happy. When we don't believe there's anything we can do about it, we feel justified in giving up. It's not a happy thing. When we can't succeed in our intimate relationship, on some level we feel like a failure.

That is only our intimate relationships. How important are the relationships between parents and their children? Are these possibly the most important relationships we have in our lives? When communication and understanding fail in relationships between kids and parents, lives can change for the worse very quickly. In America, we have been falsely taught that the relationship between teenagers and their parents is almost inevitably problematic and adversarial. While it is true that in modern American culture there has been a breakdown between the generations, especially since the 1950s, in huge numbers of families with shared values and good communication, there's no such environment of misunderstanding. In many cultures, teenagers and parents have always worked in harmony, enjoying and valuing each other's presence. What is their secret?

Let me say it again, because I really believe this is important: When we understand our needs as humans, we gain the ability to not only satisfy our own needs, but to satisfy the needs of others.

This knowledge helps us bridge the gaps of communication and understanding, reversing the negative effects we experience when we cannot make our relationships with others work.

That was a brief introduction to the needs themselves. Now we can cover some general strategy--related questions that most people have. Moving along from there, we will look at the needs again in a different way This will increase your ability to notice and use them. Occasionally I may refer to previous examples; this is done intentionally to relate an important idea more comprehensively.

As we continue, it is important to notice that everyone values and prioritizes the needs in a different order.

The needs themselves represent unconscious emotional targets that play enormous roles in our thought processes and our behavior. All of our actions can be traced back to an attempt to satisfy one or more of these needs. We must understand, though, that each of us values these needs with our own unique level of intensity and in our own order of importance. For some people the need for certainty is highest on their list, and most of the actions they take will be to gain more certainty or avoid uncertainty. Such a person will appreciate long-term stable relationships and secure employment. If the person's second highest need is love, there may be a conflict in intimate relationships. This is because intimate relationships will, at some point or other, give us plenty of uncertainty. This could cause that person to only look for certain (safe) love with children, parents, or pets and stop trying to have an intimate relationship.

Even though someone prioritizes two needs at high levels, this has no bearing on the level of satisfaction they may find for those needs. We are almost guaranteed to have some challenges satisfying them. For instance, because need processes are unconscious, some needs may be in conflict with each other. Having awareness of our needs reduces some of the challenges. There is something else to consider—the availability of ways to fill our needs: the vehicles. Having awareness of the different vehicles further reduces the challenge.

Vehicles—How We Satisfy Our Needs

We've already introduced *strategy*—our *modus operandi*—the *pattern* that tells us and the world how we operate, how we "get our groove on." One operational level below our strategy for need satisfaction is where we find the specific methods or ways in which we satisfy our needs. We will call these methods *vehicles*. We will call them vehicles because they work in a similar way to physical transportation. Just as we use a car or train to reach a destination, we use a vehicle to satisfy our emotional needs.

People have come up with countless vehicles over the years to satisfy their needs. Some of them work well, and some of them don't. Maybe they only work in certain situations. Some vehicles are positive and satisfy several needs. Good vehicle. Some vehicles satisfy needs short-term but are destructive long-term. Bad vehicle.

You are probably wondering what I mean and asking, what forms do vehicles take? Vehicles can take the form of a person's identity, or role in life, or both. This can also show up as a behavior, such as being an exercise freak or someone who continually overeats. You will easily start recognizing the different vehicles as we go.

Whatever vehicles we use, we approved them at some point because they were in line with our strategy. Sometimes, however, we don't know when or how to let go of a vehicle. If the vehicle is no longer in line with our larger goals or life plan, simple awareness that our highest good is not being served will help us ditch the vehicle and replace it with one that serves us better.

Unlike conventional physical transportation, emotional vehicles are always available to us and within us through our decisions of how to interact in the world. Because, unlike physical transportation, we are not limited by cost or availability any of us may at any time choose the equivalent of walking or riding first class in the most advanced transportation to date. Awareness of how to determine a superior vehicle is our only cost.

Chapter 9

Maps and Models

As we continue, I want to provide a little orientation on maps and models in general. I also want to share my way of thinking about how this new framework will serve you, with a unique strategies map.

We have all used a road map at some time in our lives. That makes sense; they're simple, understandable, and they work easily with the way we think. They help to make sense of and give an overview of the world. Mapping, the idea of reducing lots of information down to a few key markers, has caught on with humans because of its ease of understanding and high value of return. When we develop a map, we sort out important things, select recognizable reference points, and in some way illustrate how the points are relative to each other.

Most of the knowledge that all of us use on a day-to-day basis is a reflection of internal maps that we have and use, either consciously or unconsciously. As humans, it is ingrained in our psyches at a deep level to use maps and models, from way back in prehistory when we would make lines in the dirt with a stick to tell others where resources or dangers were. People who could use these types of maps survived; the people who could not, did not. The charting of unexplored parts of our world has always been a prioritized natural behavior of humans. By charting the seas, we were able to make sense of an unbelievably vast amount of space. To set sail with no reference points could have meant disaster. Only by slowly building on and adding reference points were we able to reduce the world down to a map that we can now hold in our hands or see on a screen. Even nowadays, the mapping and remapping continues, from the far reaches of space down to the smallest chemicals and particles in the universe—and the inner space of ourselves.

What Makes a Good Map?

A good map or model does not need to be a replica of the environment you are mapping. It does need to contain the relevant points, including any important sequences or secondary reference points. Maps and models are useful not only for what they contain, but also what they *remove* from the subject being mapped/modeled. Often we are looking at something that gives us too much information for us to process. A good diagram or map of the human circulatory system carefully removes all the elements that normally obstruct its presence.

We Already Make Maps in Our Minds

We *think* in terms of maps and models. Some refer to tangible things and we can hold them in our hands. Some, like ideas, do not. Whether the map or its referents are tangible or not, we use them to make pictures in our minds and to orient ourselves. Besides metaphors, one of the most advanced models of the intangible is, of course, the *role model*. The role model is a map or blueprint of how to be like its subject. We don't have to use every reference point a role model has to offer; context helps us to sift out the parts that we would rather not bring into our lives.

Working much like the stick in the sand, role models are great shortcuts to identifying and implementing behaviors and techniques that can greatly improve our lives. Whether we apply them in religion, business, the arts, or any other human endeavor, we are indebted to and perhaps dependent on role models. Imagine your trade or industry as if no one else had ever done it before. Can you begin to comprehend the dependence we have on the impressions that the role models of our industry have left on us? Correct or not, they are the relevant markers we use to show us where the dangers and resources are.

Drawing again from the history of psychology, we have what Carl Jung called *archetypes*. The Jung archetypes are four universal personality types: the warrior, the lover, the sage, the magician. This map was a great advance for psychotherapy. Once a client was educated about the archetypes, he could talk about, say, what the warrior within himself thought about his predicament. The archetype is a kind of role model, with reference points. Asking the advice of all the archetypes results in an expanded map and more balanced of the view of the presenting problem for the client, and brings them directly in touch with their own inner resources. That makes perfect sense. We have similar resources that are readily available to us, at any time. We might ask, what would Dad do in the situation? Or, what would Jesus do? These archetypes carry positive intents that are on at least as high a level as those of the individual who consults them.

In many intimate relationships, there are definitely times when one or both of the partners feel as though they are lost in the woods without a map. Sometimes we need a map just to help us find help! It's a tough terrain to map, with a tremendous amount of information to sort through. Professionals have yet to agree on which maps are best for relationships. Confusion and theories abound as to both cause and solution of marital difficulties, focusing on personal history, family culture, parenting styles, abuse or trauma, environment, intelligence level, emotional intelligence, and on and on. Though there are many maps from various therapy schools, usable action plans are hard to find. Though they all have some value, and are thus still being used and refined, they tend to contradict one another, don't always work, and take inordinate amounts of time to implement. Not only that; many are extremely complex and require technical understanding at a level beyond most of us.

What are unhappy individuals and couples to do? We must have accessible and usable information. We cannot always wait for therapy to work, if it ever does. To access the help we need, it is important to understand how we process information. By our very nature we are self-diagnosing. We are constantly evaluating our own level of function. If someone does not believe they understand the reason for the advice (at some level) they will naturally resist. We are served best when we recognize this fact and work towards improving personal understanding with change work.

Even if we have access to professionals, if they have not mapped out in terms we understand the best way for us to maintain our lives at our desired level of success, we seek out what is available and what seems to make sense. Because of this, stereotypes and entertaining maps have become popularized. Women are not from Venus, and men are not from Mars. Yet as a simple map, that planetary metaphor does make some sense to help us figure out where the resources and dangers are. Most importantly, it is in the hands of the people who are evaluating what's going on in their own lives and attempting to make improvements. When a map like that comes along, people get excited, because on some level it works; it helps them make better decisions and have reference points that don't require specialized training to use. So while some of these models are helpful on some level, many of them don't offer much more then anecdotal evidence.

Creating a Strategies Map

Key-strategy and needs-lock ideas, as mapped out in the chapters ahead, is an easily understandable map that we can apply in all sorts of different situations with a variety of people with all sorts of backgrounds. By simply knowing which of the needs someone values most and what their strategies are, we can assist them at a meaningful level.

Remember that if you feel uncomfortable with your understanding of the material at any time during reading, relax, you only need to keep reading and that will unfold the rest of the map for you so that you can enjoy a full picture.

Stories of senseless harm to oneself and others are prevalent throughout the American media, and I think when we hear these stories we ask ourselves, why would someone do that? Why or how is it they did not see that they had other options? Certainly any drive we have to help others stems from our idea that we can help them see options that they don't. It's obvious to us that it is a better choice to leave an embroiled family situation rather than physically harming anyone.

I can tell you from much experience that the sad truth is that when people are at their wits' end, they have no confidence that doing something else will make a difference. They believe they are like the key that's already been cut. They have been trying a lifetime to conform in a way that will satisfy their needs, and they no longer believe that the lock will open for them. At that point, reasonable alternatives seem to be to take some extreme action and either destroy themselves (the key), or their immediate environment where they are attempting to satisfy the needs (the lock).

Understanding our core strategies and mapping them out in a simple key-lock metaphor brings into focus many complicated hidden motivations behind our behavior. If we are honest, we will admit that there have been times when we have not felt loved enough, or certain or validated enough. This understanding will help you reshape your strategy, helping yourself and others to open those locks in positive ways.

I classify the strategy as a key or master need. That is to say, I believe it is a need in the truest sense, plus some special characteristics. I believe it is perhaps something we experience that is just beyond our ability to describe it. A close approximation might be to say that it is our "sense of being" it is the total of everything that makes us what we believe we are.

Unlike the other needs, we will always experience this need at a 10; in fact, we experience it more strongly when we are not satisfying our other needs because our strategy is supposed to open the lock.

I added validation to the strategy map because I believe it to be one of the strongest influencers with someone's strategy. Additionally, if you were to do nothing but help other people feel validated, it is likely you would simultaneously unlock both your needs. Validation is a mutually rewarding experience.

I added goals to the needs classification, not so much because they are as high a drive as significance, love, validation, but rather, because I believe when we choose to value goals and purpose highly, our lives are automatically elevated in a fulfilling way.

It was not my first instinct to change or alter in any way the extremely useful human needs models. After all, these models are indeed great and *who am I?* After a long cost-benefit analysis on the subject and some self validation, I concluded that the continued evolution of these basic needs models only adds choices and serves everyone best. This evolution includes maintaining credit to those who have brought the technology this far. I believe that is important.

Confusion is a downside of making too many unnecessary changes. Some other options were to place the additional needs at a different levels or values. Changing the value of the additional needs, making them different, at first seemed like a good idea, except that there is already a hierarchal interpretation challenge with the needs. By that I mean the needs are being presented like a map without restrictions on how someone may use the map. People have had a tendency to look at the needs and want to place values or impose some sort of sequence (believing some needs are "better" than others). These natural sorting tendencies can cause problems with application or outcomes. It's true that the needs do have different characteristics but proper sorting is done relative to how each individual values them rather than a universal valuation.

The issue with predetermining a value is one of interpretation. Here's what I mean. When someone creates and publishes a road map of the United States, their considerations are to provide a useful overview of the territory. Road maps, we know, do not suggest a limited use or require a destination. Depending on design, the maps are flexible; they accommodate different people in any number of circumstances. The map may include features beyond actual roads, such as landmarks, restaurants, service stations, and parks. It is not up to the map maker to decide its use or suggest that the location of parks is more important than the location of service stations. Values judgments or rankings are best determined based on outcomes of the user. Without knowing the outcome, we cannot know the level of importance of individual features.

A true test of map is, of course, usefulness. If it can serve someone in getting a positive outcome or understanding, then it has value. I believe all the previous popularized behavioral maps (not based on needs) became so because of some level of usefulness, and for that their originators should be recognized favorably. This map you are now holding in your hands (or seeing on some screen) is an accumulation of years of work of some very skilled mapmakers from different fields, along with some additions and interconnections that I have added based on thousands of hours of study and practice. Even so, this map is not absolutely equivalent to the circumstances and situations it is mapping. (It is not a replica.) Human behavior is very complex (perhaps never 100% replicable), and for my purposes an elegant, simplified, useful map that anyone can understand and brings awareness of resources and dangers is the desired goal.

Chapter 10

Understanding Is Key—Everybody Loves Their Strategy

Start with yourself.

By starting with yourself, you can more fully experience the universal truths of how the needs affect each of us.

Anthony Robbins will have people do a little exercise where they identify a task that they just love and that other people typically hate. Usually it will be something like cleaning the house, or bookkeeping, or working on the car. Then he will ask them to rate on a scale of 1 to 10 how effective that task is at satisfying each of the six needs that he has identified. Let's take as an example a woman who says she loves to clean house. Here's that person's typical results. On the certainty scale, she is likely to have given it an 8, 9, or 10. She is likely to say that she has great confidence in her ability to do a good job (usually better than anyone else—she knows what to do, how to do it, how long it will take, and so on). She will give similarly high ratings to variety, for reasons such as that with four children there is always something unexpected to deal with, and to significance, because she is doing a great job at performing a function that is very important to her family. It turns out that the rest of the needs are likely to rank right up there: growth, because she is always learning better and faster ways to get the house clean, and contribution, because she provides an exceptional environment for her family. Love and connection, again high, because she feels loving connection as she irons the kids clothing, she also connects with her Creator through prayer.

So those are the results based on Tony's six needs. Tony teaches that any behavior that meets three or more needs at high levels (6 to 10) will be addictive. Clearly this example is in the addictive category. What would our housecleaning-loving woman say if we asked her to rate herself on needs seven through nine? Just for fun, let's try it.

- Goal, outcome, or result. Clearly there is a desired outcome that she targets and achieves—a clean and livable house, for sure, and maybe some others that you can think of.

- Validation. Perhaps this person grew up in a very clean household, and she saw her mother get praise and favorable attention from friends and family for her housekeeping abilities. We could assume she would give herself eight or nine because she knows her mom would be proud of the way she keeps her house.

- Strategy. Predictably she would score herself high as having an excellent strategy for satisfying her own needs and being an exemplary type of person. Likely at some point she decided that being a good housekeeper would be an excellent vehicle to satisfy her needs. This decision probably took place at an early age as a result of some experience with a role model with whom she identified or wished to be like—perhaps her mother or aunt or even someone on TV. Whether she's aware of it or not, this strategy is certainly something that she has decided on and willingly does to align with people in a favorable way.

Not all the scores need to be this high for someone to love an activity as though it were part of their identity. Just satisfying three or four needs at high levels can do the trick.

Now it's your turn! Think of something you really enjoy doing and that you are good at. Now run through each of the nine needs and rate on a scale of 1 to 10 how much this activity satisfies those needs. I predict that doing this for your favorite activity will show you that you satisfy at least five or six of those needs at seven or above. If you chose an activity that you *really* like and are *really* good at it, I predict you will rate even higher than that.

Now let's do the opposite and have you pick something you just cannot stand to do. Something that other people don't mind or even like to do. Something that makes you cringe at the thought of the onerous task; you would gladly pay someone else good money to do it for you. I know you can think of something. Got it? Good! Rate yourself, on a scale of 1 to 10 . . .

How significant do you feel when you're doing it?
How much certainty does it provide for you?
How much variety do you experience by doing this task?
How much love and connection do you experience when doing this task?
How much growth do you feel when doing this task?
How much contribution you feel when doing this task?
How validated do you feel when you have to do this? (Hint: Would you like others to see you doing this?)
How excited are you about accomplishing the goal of this task? (No, I don't mean just getting the heck out of there.)
How much does it feel like your plan for life is working when you do this?

Anyone can predict these scores are going to be pretty dismal. Although you may be able to satisfy a few needs at high levels doing this disgusting thing, for the most part I think you'll find that the tasks you hate and do not want to do are the ones that do not satisfy any or many needs, even if the tasks serve you in some way.

These examples are important. They show us that our motivation to do things, or not to do things, operates without our conscious awareness, and can be understood by these needs. By the same token, we can understand some of the actions, motivations and intentions of others, even when they themselves may not. These tools and understandings can be very important in areas where we deal with other people.

We All Love Our Strategies

Whenever we do something, we do it because it "feels right." We have needs that drive everything we do—even if we cannot always say what they are. We all have certain special, unique things that we do repeatedly to fill these needs. These actions seem *appropriate* to us. We don't have to even think about *why* we do them—we just do them. That special pattern is called our strategy.

Why do the actions that make up our strategy seem appropriate to us? There are seven billion strategies in the world, and of all those, our own seems the best. It all goes back to the history of our complex nervous system. Ultimately it is our nervous system and what it has learned to associate with pleasure and pain that makes the decision of what is appropriate and consistent with our strategy for satisfying of all of our needs. Let's take a silly example of an action that either is, or is not, part of different people's strategies: donating $100 to a local charity.

- I donate because when I do kind things, I experience positive inner feelings. I may even get into heaven because of it. (It is part of the person's strategy for inner peace with herself and her Creator—a source of pleasure.)
- I donate because I think of myself as a kind person and it makes me feel good to be seen that way. If I do not donate, people might believe me to be unkind, and that would be painful. (Being a kind person is part of the person's strategy for making people think well of her, and it feels good.)
- I feel bad and guilty most of the time, and donating makes me feel a little better about myself. (Perhaps she knows her overall strategy is unfair in some way to others and she wants to compensate.)
- I resist donating because I have been severely criticized for wasting my money on helping others who don't deserve it; donating is painful because it makes me feel foolish. (Not donating is part of the person's strategy for being seen as wise and

thus more acceptable, at least to those who value that type of wisdom, also perhaps avoiding the pain of feeling judged.)

The same action of making, or avoiding making, a donation, has a different basis for each person who does it. Yet if you were to question any of the above actions, suggest that what the person did was not appropriate, you might get some unpleasant push-back. You may have thought that you were providing an opportunity for the person to review their decision about that action calmly and rationally, with your kind help. What you were really doing was questioning the result of that person's having used his or her strategy as a sounding board for action. Remember, strategy is deep, deployed mostly unconsciously, and often seen by the person as part of his or her identity. So, when you question a person's action, what the person thought was appropriate, you are often stepping on toes big time. When you thought you were only questioning a simple decision and action, you were really going after the person's entire strategy, and he or she took it as a personal affront, even rejection by you.

Strategy is NOT our identity.

It is NOT our beliefs.

It is NOT our values, actions, or behaviors.

We might as well quote *Webster's* 11th here, because it fits: "Strategy is . . . a careful plan or method . . . an adaptation or complex of adaptations . . . as of behavior. . that serves . . . an important function in achieving evolutionary success." (Well, it fits as long as we notice that strategies are not always consciously deployed.)

Though our unique identity, beliefs, values, actions, and behaviors are not our strategy, they are often confused with it. At best these things are only influenced by our strategy. They change as we use our strategy to interpret our ever-changing and unique circumstances in life.

A major key to changing strategies or unwanted behavior lies in noticing the distinctions between these groups that we normally roll into one.

How Strategies Begin

Our strategies develop when we are children. If we do not update them, they can operate continuously throughout our lives, and we may even pass them on to our own children. Understanding what strategy you or anyone else used as a child can be discovered fairly easily by answering this question: Who did you need to be to get attention and love from the most important people in your environment when you were a child (this was likely one or both of your parents). Did you need to be cute, funny, smart? On the contrary, were you rewarded only when you kept quiet and did your chores without complaining? Did your engineer dad encourage you when you started building bridges with building blocks? Was Mom a ballerina when she was little and loved it when you pirouetted around the house in your tutu?

It is not surprising that our families have a pronounced affect the strategies we use: It is the environment of our initial development. The ways that we believed were best to be successful at satisfying our needs in that environment start to become generalized for us. We begin to feel and believe this is how we should be in life.

It is also not surprising that our parents want to pass on their own strategies. All people, including parents, believe that their strategy is the best way that a human being could possibly be and want to pass this important tool on to their kids. If the parents confuse their strategy with their own identity, they will be especially pleased if the kids accept the strategy as their own, and will likely feel upset, rejected, and invalidated, should the child reject the strategy.

Many parents reject a child who breaks family tradition by forging a new path in life. This parental behavior makes perfect sense when you take out your map and apply the idea of strategies. The parents, and probably the family structure present and past, have supported a certain set of strategies that they believe to be the best a person can do. In their minds, for the child to reject those strategies would be foolish. They may reject the child by withdrawing emotional or financial support in the hopes that the child will see how important it is to them that the child follow the parental strategy. If they have confused their strategy with their identity, they will feel justified in their rejection, believing that the child rejected them first.

Other parents may not be so controlling if they operate on a more liberal strategy themselves. They may encourage the child to be someone who is true to herself, or does the best he can, or decides for herself and operates from the heart.

In either case, the child will need to decide whether accepting or rejecting the strategy rewarded by these significant people is the best course. Often among siblings, there will be a split between children regarding acceptance and rejection of the strategies. If, say, the first child is already the good child who receives attention and recognition for most closely accepting the strategy the parent gives rewards for, then, because of an underlying need to be unique and special (significant), the second child may reject the strategy and become reinforced in doing so, because she will receive much more attention than the cooperative child. Although it is a potentially destructive strategy, the rebellious behavior, though it seemingly overrides common sense, will continue to be felt by the rebel as an "appropriate" action because it is satisfying other needs than being accepted, particularly significance. (This is important to understand, because it explains why many people seem addicted to rebellious or destructive behavior and have trouble changing, even when they know better.)

Examples of Strategies

Depression. In some cases (certainly not all) feelings of helplessness and depression can be a strategy. If we are feeling sad or hopeless or depressed as a small child, people come to us and give us all sorts of love and attention and support. Part of us may link these facts up: Hey, this is a good deal. I complain and people respond. I get special treats or some other privilege. Maybe even this is a way for me to know who really loves me, because anyone who really loves me will be supportive and helpful when I am down and out. In psychology this is known as secondary gain. (Consciously, of course, and thinking in a grownup fashion, we would not accept such a strategy, because it doesn't take in the bigger picture, and we like to believe that we would notice when we are taking advantage of people and would like to think we have more than one way to determine if somebody loves us.)

Smoking. As with the previous example, thinking logically is not how we come up with strategies. If that were true, then we would have no problem giving up cigarettes once we understand that they are bad for us. We don't consciously decide that we are going to keep smoking. It is how we *emotionalize* our strategy: the emotions we experience when we think about or run the strategy that includes smoking. If we feel good when we think about it or do it, we will maintain our desire to keep doing it. For instance, if we smoke because we believe it makes us appear sexually appealing or sophisticated to our peer group, then we will resist giving up that strategy/value/identity. It's best to notice there is much more to smoking than just being addicted to nicotine. There is another addiction: to our belief that this behavior is satisfying our needs for (and they are different for everyone) significance, validation, variety, connection, certainty/comfort, and so on. These beliefs around our needs are sometimes automatic, when our role models use the strategy of smoking, we may take on their addiction with certainty of it's value as a vehicle.

Cultural positions. One of the best examples of what a strategy is and how much people love them was given in a sitcom from the 1970s. It was the earthy yet sophisticated television show *All in the Family* that revolutionized American TV by dealing with issues previously not deemed appropriate for television. The show centered on two characters in constant conflict: the antihero Archie Bunker and his live-in son-in-law Michael ("Meathead"). Both characters represented strong, inflexible, and polar-opposite strategies based on two cultural positions that were, at the time, exaggerated mirrors of strategies and viewpoints of large segments of the American population. Many episodes of the show revolved around Archie and Mike fruitlessly attempting to display the faults in the other strategy and convert the other one to their point of view. In my mind, the show did a very good job of not only showing what strategies are but also demonstrating how people cling onto their strategies, even when the light of common sense is cast upon them.

Why We Need Strategies

As I've said before, for us to function normally, we need to think and feel that we know what we are doing and that we can succeed. When we don't believe this about ourselves in one or more areas of life, or our overall life, we will experience emotional pain.

If you are in an intimate relationship and there are problems (trouble with emotions, understanding, or communication) and you do not know what to do, can you be happy? Very doubtful. Gen. Semantics founder, Alfred Korzybski suggests that you have an ideal picture (or map) of how your life should be in order for you to be happy, but your actual life doesn't match the ideal picture in many or most ways. You will feel emotional pain. Well, if you have a strategy to bridge that gap, and you know you can implement it, you will feel much better than you would with no workable strategy at all. Simply put, if you don't know how to get your life to match your ideal picture, your pain will move to a stronger level.

Strategies Need to Evolve!

Our strategies are meant to satisfy our needs. We believe they are the best ways to satisfy our needs. For most people, though, they rarely work really well, and when they do work, it is usually in a limited way, with only a few relationships and in limited contexts.

Here's an odd thing though: When our strategies are not working, we do not usually change them! Rather, we usually intensify and become more intrenched in the behavior that is not working. If we can, we leave that area and spend more time in areas where our strategy *does* work and less time in areas where things are clearly not working and where we are not positively reinforced for our amazing abilities.

Here's another odd thing: We are much more willing to expand our behavior and try new strategies when things are going well and we are succeeding at satisfying our needs. It seems the comfort of our success empowers us to try new things. When we are failing to satisfy our needs, we become stressed and we are more likely to intensify the exact behavior that isn't working: overeating, drug use, self-imposed isolation, self-pity, blaming others. When we are stressed, we are less likely to think clearly and more likely to intensify the behavior that is causing the problem. For many, after years of intense negative behavior, family and friends cut off contact and the person is left alone in pain. This is a pattern run by a majority of repeat callers to crisis lines.

The opposite of evolving needs is blocking them. We can understand a great deal about violent or self-destructive behavior when we trace it back to a belief by the violent person that either their environment or someone in it is blocking their needs. I am saying that if someone is behaving violently or threatening us, we can almost certainly trace it to this type of cause.

In normal healthy development, our strategies need to be updated and modified for our ever-changing set of contexts and life stage or age. One key time frame is adolescence, where we stop caring so much about what our parents think, and we stop focusing on strategies to gain their emotional acceptance. During this stage there is very little more relevant to a child than how they believe they are perceived by their peers. They will take drastic steps to gain acknowledgment as being worthy of emotional acceptance by others in the group they identify with. The strategy they use to receive this emotional acceptance may be positive or negative. It may work really well, or it may backfire and leave the child feeling isolated. A great example of this is when a child acts on a decision to shift the area in which they are meeting their needs, parents to peers and such. There's a sense of vulnerability when we open up with romantic feelings towards someone. Should the person we open up to reject us, we may place several negative meanings on it. We may feel invalidated at an identity and strategy level, also meaning that our strategies for meeting our needs in intimate relationships are not working. If the rejection becomes public, the negative meanings can intensify, especially if the result is rejection by a large portion of a person's peer group. Teenage suicide following disclosure of same-sex preferences that resulted in rejection and harassment from others is a very poignant example of this failure to shift the way in which needs are being met. Without awareness of what is happening, should an emotional backfiring occur, there is not much the child or anyone else can do. At this point, without confidence in their needs-meeting strategy, there is an elevated risk of suicide. Why would backfiring of a strategy have such a drastic result?

For many reasons. Everyone loves their own strategy. Parents are willing to disown their children because of their belief in their own strategy. We often confuse the strategy we use with our identity. The fact that the strategy and its backfiring occur outside of conscious awareness leads us to believe there is nothing we can do, accompanied by thoughts and feelings such as, *I'm a failure. I have this great strategy but it doesn't work in this world. The strategy worked for me before in some way and now it doesn't. I don't know what to do and I cannot connect a meaningful way with others. Maybe I should end it all.*

However, when we understand strategies and how and when to change them, better options open up.

Interesting Facts About Strategies

Strategy, Identity and Vehicle Can Be Intertwined. So what strategy do we use to feel worthy within whatever relationships we have with others? We all have at least one strategy, and usually a few, that are somewhat intertwined or confused with our sense of identity. Many people use identification with their career as a primary strategy. They can say, "I went to So-and-so College and now I am a doctor, a lawyer, or a university president (vehicle as identity). Their career may end up being the basis for their identity, and to a large extent others will make assumptions about them based on their occupation or career.

Perhaps you dislike your occupation and don't wish to have it be your identity at all. Well, then you might wish to make yourself known as "someone who would rather be . . . building houses, or saving the world, or living in France." Some identify with interests or hobbies. We like to do the things that are in tune with how we would like to be perceived in the world. Do we race cars, or are we more into Zen meditation? Do we read certain kinds of books that differentiate us? For others, the strategy is to talk about the glory days when at some point in their life they proved in some way that they were worthy, even though they aren't necessarily contributing a lot at present. They wear those past deeds as a badge reflecting their identity/value, and they want to tell you all about it.

Role Models Can Contain Prepackaged Strategies. Usually we adopt a strategy without even understanding it. Role models may have a strategy built into them. Think about it. Picture a role model that you would like to resemble as close as possible. Imagine the actions, values, beliefs, and identity needed to be like this person. Could you copy them, and is it compelling for you to do so? Have you ever seen this happen? (Hint: Note how some people get of-fended or fight when a favorite role model is criticized.)

Ideological Positions Can Provide Strategies. Do you belong to an ideologically oriented group or political party? At the level of commitment you feel is "appropriate," do you find that you are provided with a clear understanding of beliefs and values, the actions you should take because of your alignment? The group's understanding of beliefs and values can give you a sense of identity—a shortcut for decision-making and behavior that you end up perceiving as "true to yourself." You can even develop a partial strategy just by opposing or rejecting a group or political party.

Global Beliefs Affect Strategies. A global belief is a large generalization we make about big areas of our life or environment: All people are generally goodhearted. People respect authority. These broad statements we make to ourselves will influence how we apply our strategy. Someone may have a global belief that financially successful attorneys have a fabulous life that satisfies most human needs. Perhaps a person selects a profession with a title like Doctor, Professor, or CEO for the same reason. If so, it is likely the person may play-up the doctor or CEO strategy and capitalize on its perceived status to satisfy as many needs as possible. The strategy may work well in a number of situations, and yet it may turn out that even doctors have troubled children or bad marriages and that a good percentage of the population may resent them and their wealth and skills. If that happens, the person might overgeneralize and conclude that most people cannot appreciate this wonderful strategy, and begin to isolate from the general populace, spending more time socializing with others who share the same strategy.

Strategies Can Be Affiliations. Another important strategy is who we align with and why. Do we have friends in high places, or do we have friends in awfully low places? Do we show our values to the world by having a trophy spouse? Do we know important people and go to important functions, or do we sit with children at a local cancer hospital? Do we avoid all people because our strategy is to be aware of the vast array of human imperfections, and by disowning them all, display our higher value?

Our strategy is very personal for us because it is our perspective on the best decision process and course of action required for us to feel certain we can satisfy our needs. Therefore it is understandable why we are so very protective (as we would be toward any lifeline) and cling to it. It is the single basket that holds all of our prized emotional eggs.

Chapter 11

The Strategy Is There to Serve Us

Whether we are addicted to a strategy of going into depression or something physical like smoking cigarettes, it is because we associate satisfying most or all of our needs to that activity. We usually feel we are satisfying those needs at high levels. When we first started the behavior or activity, we found that it satisfied one or more needs, and that is why it became addictive. After some time, though, the pattern usually shifts, and the level of satisfaction, as well as the specific needs that are met, can change.

Let's take smoking. (Well, let's not, but you know what I mean.) When you first start, you may say (after the initial pain), I have certainty that I will feel a certain way, a pleasant familiar state, likely where I can relax and breathe freely. I'm certain others will view me favorably (just like in the ads). Later you may find more needs that smoking satisfies. It could work for variety, because when I stand out on the street to have a smoke, I never know what will happen or who I will see out there. I may feel love or connection with myself for taking some "me time" and doing something for myself, just because I want to. I may feel significant because I've escaped the pressure to quit that everyone else has given in to, and now I remain true to myself. Big accomplishment, right? I may feel validated that I am doing the right thing. I and other smokers need to stick together for what we believe is right in the face of legislators and taxing agents who are out to get us. I may have a goal to prove I can smoke four packs a day and still live to be 100 years old. My strategy as a smoker allows me to grow and contribute by emulating positive figures who smoked as part of their image, such as the Rat Pack, the Beatles, or any other people who experienced admiration and acclaim while using cigarettes to solidify that image.

When someone is convinced they're receiving all of these positive benefits from an activity, it's no wonder that they will want to continue doing it! This means that anyone who has quit smoking successfully has changed their emotionalized view of the behavior relative to need satisfaction. For example:

· They are certain it will kill them soon; it threatens survival.
· Too much variety in wondering who will be the next person to look down on them for being too weak to give up such a stupid habit.
· By dying young, they will lose the love and connection with the people most important to them, and they will not get to experience being around their children and grandchildren.
· They will stop feeling significant sneaking around like a criminal in unglamorous places just to have a smoke.
· They realize that only by being alive and changing can they truly grow, contribute, and employ a strategy that is beneficial for themselves and others.

Not everyone will be motivated by the same reasons to stop and start various actions, of course; we all have different triggers that will affect us differently. The triggers to change behavior do need to work in relation (like a key and lock) to the nine needs. Those specific triggers are based on our values and beliefs and conditioning. Typically though, we consider stopping a bad habit or other unwanted behavior because it no longer satisfies all of our needs at high levels or in positive ways. When this happens, we experience mixed feelings about the behavior. This results in inner conflict and our attempt to consciously weigh the advantages and disadvantages of the behavior. If we don't stop, it is because the behavior satisfies enough of our needs, and so we will tend to ignore or minimize negative aspects of it.

Motivation is always needs driven. People tend to focus more on the areas of their life where their needs matter and focus less on areas where they do not. Focus can happen in different areas of our lives and in areas besides addictions.

Some principal areas of focus or categories are . . .

· Self-care and development
· Intimate relationships
· Career
· Hobbies and other specialized interests
· Relationships with friends and family

If someone is not satisfying their needs in their intimate relationship, they will seek to satisfy their needs elsewhere. Perhaps through work, hobbies, friends, or family. Worse yet, they may give up and start to satisfy their needs in negative ways.

Someone may stay in a job, relationship, or situation that does not satisfy their needs because changing that situation would go against or threaten other needs. So they might stick it out while being unhappy with their job, or if it's a relationship, cheating on their partner. We can quickly uncover the real problem by discovering which needs are being met negatively at the expense of the ones not believed capable of being satisfied positively.

We have a need to have a strategy for achieving the most important things in our lives. It is truly a need, and without it we will experience a range of very negative feelings or emotions.

So in a sense, the overall strategy is how we organize the other eight needs and includes our vehicle use for satisfying those needs. In the previous example, smoking was a vehicle to satisfy several needs. Being a doctor is a vehicle to satisfy needs. We all use vehicles to satisfy our needs; this is a subset or building block, if you will, of our larger or core strategy. A hint at determining if a behavior is a subset of someone's core strategy would be that they link the behavior with an identity; I am a smoker, I am a doctor, I am depressed, I am a comedian.

If you're at all confused, remember it is likely because most of us tend to lump together identity, strategy, behavior, and vehicles. Remember to notice them as being different so you can understand yourself and others much more accurately.

Career-focused Needs Conflicts

Many of us experience needs conflicts in our careers. Two common examples are . . .

- We like the status of our position (significance), but the pay isn't that great.
- We like the pay because it gives a great deal of certainty in our lives, but we don't like the way we are treated because it takes away from our feeling of significance.

You could ask yourself, what do I like most about my career? Is it the title, the pay, the variety, my chance to grow and contribute, some certainty other than pay, the love connection and validation of people in my working environment? Strong sense of mission and goal, or perhaps the great system that the organization uses? Which of the needs are *not* fulfilled through your career? Have you experienced inner conflict because of conflicting needs?

Year after year, surveys have revealed that job satisfaction has less to do with pay then most employers realize. This makes sense too. If you give someone a lot of money but put them in an environment where they are ridiculed or invalidated, and then take away all certainty regarding the position, make them feel insignificant, give them no clear goal and no way to achieve it, have them repeat it over and over and over without variety, take away all love and connection with other people, then you will see how long they are going to be happy employees. If you pay them some totally obscene dollar amount, they may stick it out and satisfy their needs in other areas of their life until they can clear out of this situation. When you think about it, though, with that kind of money they must feel pretty significant, and will certainly be able to imagine ways they can satisfy all their needs. That shows how the motivation is still needs driven.

Relationship-focused Needs

When someone's marriage or relationship is ending, the same type of language is used by everyone. They say things like, "I don't know what to do. I have tried everything. Nothing works." Translation: I don't have a workable strategy or plan to reach my outcome with this person.

(NOTE: This is our viewpoint for giving up on all sorts of activities or relationships we become involved with. We don't know how to get along with our kids or our parents. We don't know how to succeed in becoming financially independent. If we had a strategy that we believed would work, we would not experience the emotional pain that we have without the strategy. More than just a framework for satisfying needs, the strategy itself is a need.)

Many people are skeptical of relationships or marriage. They feel that because so many marriages end in divorce, it may be better to just avoid it. This is a reflection of their confidence in the strategy they have regarding relationships. Someone very confident in their ability to maintain a positive relationship will be confident in committing to marriage, and someone who feels that relationships are uncontrollable and unpredictable will prefer to avoid them. Here's the kicker: Our feeling about our strategy is what allows us to take action, and it has nothing to do with how good our strategy really is. Paul McCartney, in his second marriage, to Heather Mills, elected to not sign a prenuptial agreement. It was clear that he was very confident in his relationship strategy and had no concern that he did not have the skills to maintain the relationship. Despite contrary advice from several people, Paul trusted his strategy for maintaining the marriage. In fact, it is likely that part of his strategy was to clearly exhibit that sort of confidence and trust in his partner. He likely understood that displaying distrust of someone in that high-level kind of a relationship would certainly be a poor idea. Ultimately though, the couple was unable to satisfy the rest of each other's needs long-term.

Developing Need-fulfilling Strategies

As we saw in the example of a high-paying job where someone may endure a situation because it satisfies one or two needs, the person will look in other categories of their life to satisfy the rest of their needs.

By using a map that clarifies our need structures, we have an ability to understand and enhance appropriate strategies that allow the realization of our best intentions from where we are now. This based on areas where we do know what to do and how to make things work. From there we can create more enjoyable strategies in areas that require our involvement, as well as enhancing areas we are involved with by our own preference.

Chapter 12

An Achievable Goal or Outcome

The second step to having successful evaluation processes is to realize that you absolutely need to have a goal.

The right goal can put purpose and meaning in our lives; it can inspire us in countless ways. Great leaders have inspired millions with their visions of worthwhile goals that people could rally around and take action for their own benefit and for the greater good. A leader in any context must be able to communicate a high goal vision for the group, and the methods and values by which the goal will be obtained. In business this is called a company's mission statement. It is a clear communication justifying the business's existence and describing what its goals are and how they are to be accomplished. A good mission statement is a good sounding board for the thought processes of the individual and of groups within the organization for making decisions in line with the business's overall purpose and strategy. The goal works well, whether it is used by one person or by a collective group of any size. A mission statement also clarifies for customers, suppliers, vendors, competition, or anyone else affected by the business what they can expect in dealing with the business or its staff.

The same principle applies to you as an individual. Without the essential element of a goal, our thought processes would be merely random neural firings—reactions, worries, idle chattering—what Buddhists call the Monkey Mind, or a horse, if you will, galloping off in eight directions all at once.

A goal starts to put our mental processes into action. It is an essential sounding board in our to and fro evaluation process. Not having a goal is like trying to play Ping-Pong without the table.

Before goals, we have questions. A question starts our evaluation process. If we break down the evaluation process, it is nothing more than us internally asking and answering questions. When we start asking questions, obviously we have some sort of goal, or we wouldn't be asking the question. But it isn't necessarily a clear goal. If we bring our goal to awareness, speak it out loud, then our evaluation process can begin with really good questions, such as, how do I reach this goal? Is the goal realistic? These are great questions because they have a definite target as a reference point. Do not ask questions such as "Why do I never reach my goals?" That question has a meaningless reference point and has nothing to do with getting your goal.

This leads to an important point you should definitely take away with you from this book.

The difference in your goal outcome is dramatically shaped by whether you ask a positive or negative question.

Let's try it. Ask yourself this question: How can I be so stupid?

What answers did you get? You probably came up with a long list of stupid things you've done. (I know it's not hard for me to come up with a list like that.) But how empowered did it make you feel? Maybe you're not even stupid. But like the old saying goes: Ask a stupid question, get a stupid answer.

Try a better-phrased question: How did I learn so much in my life?

What answers did you get? Did you start fondly remembering important learning experiences and helpful people? How empowered do you feel now? You can consciously shape your internal evaluation process by asking questions that relate to a positive outcome.

Let's sample some progressively better ways of asking the same question and notice the internal evaluation process for each. Before you begin, think of a goal that you would like to reach.

1. Why can't I stick to my goals?

_____

_____

2. How can I reach my goals?

_____

_____

3. How many different ways can I think of to reach my goal?

_____

_____

4. How can I have fun and involve my family or friends to reach this goal?

_____

_____

5. Could I reach this goal easily? If I could, how would I do it?

_____

_____

6. How can I easily satisfy my top two or three needs while I reach this outcome?

_____

_____

You should have experienced more relevant positive answers towards really achieving your outcome as you work your way through the list. I did change at question 3 from "goals" to "goal," and I hope you noticed that the thought process becomes much easier the more specific your goal is. If your question is general and not defined, your answer will be too.

Notice too that the first word of your answer can give you insight into the process as related to goals. On the "why" question, your answer probably started with the word "because." This happens when the question isn't asking for a solution, only asking for you to identify the obstruction. "Because" answers will not reveal the steps needed to reach your goal. Though they may identify challenges on the path, they must be followed up with questions that give direct solutions relating to outcome.

Not Just Any Old Goal

Be careful what you wish for. This old saying is especially true in the area of goals.

- Be clear! Say exactly what it is you want. Poorly stated or otherwise distorted goals make a distorted or otherwise irrelevant sounding board.
- Be positive! State your goal in terms of what you DO want, not what you don't want. You don't need the image of what is not wanted cluttering up your evaluation process.
- Avoid obstacles in your goal. Don't say, "I need to learn what is keeping me from having money." Say instead, "How can I experience more abundance now?" You don't want your evaluation process to include noticing things that match up with being broke.
- Have a realistic goal. Goals based on whether they are achievable or realistic will be evaluated much differently than goals that we feel are unlikely or unachievable. We will make different decisions about realistic goals than about those we know are too far off or pie-in-the-sky to ever happen.
- Include your needs into your goal statement. If we consider need satisfaction in our goal, we will increase our effectiveness at reaching them dramatically.

Goal Setting in Marriage

"Having a great marriage and staying together happily married your entire lives" is a positive and clearly stated goal. Consider all your needs in stating this goal, and if you also consider your partners emotional needs, you can have as an additional goal making sure your partner also feels their needs are met at high levels.

You will likely experience your goal almost right away. If your partner feels loved, if you bring him or her fun and variety, make them feel important and significant, appreciate them and validate their identity, and support their goals of growth and contribution, and you share a strategy of satisfying one another's needs, well, this would be an amazing relationship. Robbins suggests that when someone feels that their needs are truly being met with their partner in this way, they will never want to leave the relationship.

He say's, in the beginning, most relationships are like that because the partners are excited enough to commit to making the partner feel satisfaction of several of these needs at high levels. Then there is often a decline in the understanding of how important it is to make sure that your partner's needs are met first, especially the top ones. Even in really good relationships that last, only a few of these needs may be being satisfied at high levels. Usually people only satisfy the needs at high levels that they themselves value most. This happens to work in a relationship when the couple share a strong desire for the same needs. In that way they can understand what the other person wants.

If they both value love and certainty as their top two needs, they will have an appreciation for each other and similar things. Even if they both value and pursue different sorts of goals in life, they still can be in harmony with each other based on their need structures.

Whether we value the needs similar to our partner's or not, what we must watch out for is the tendency to try to satisfy our own needs first. This can lead to a feeling of emotional scarcity, and can show up as some form of struggle. For example: If one of the people in a relationship feels that their partner does not love them enough for their own needs to be met, they may tell the partner or others that they are not feeling loved enough. Let's face it, when we feel unloved, our typical reaction is not to want to bury our partner with love. More commonly, we feel we should match our partners level of love. We justify this with several reasons. It seems to make sense that if our partner is not satisfying our need for love, that if we give a hint and match what they are doing, they will recognize the problem and become more loving. Or we may feel vulnerable in some way, giving more love than we are receiving. If both partners use this strategy, there will be a pattern of reduced positive emotions.

Or the tendency in relationships to satisfy the need we value highest, expecting our partner to experience a positive emotional state according to what we believe should be. Yet this will not work if we value love and connection most and our partner needs to feel that they are significant and appreciated for their contributions before they allow themselves to feel loved and connected on a meaningful emotional level.

Goals and Identity

Remember, a marriage contract sounds impersonal. Yet it can be a great tool for defining roles and goals; it is similar to a mission statement. It clarifies a new identity with certain outcomes and procedures for the couple. It also serves to put others on notice of the relationship and commitment to each other, so that they may treat those individuals in a way supportive of those goals. In other words, everyone understands that a spouse will stop dating eligible singles once they are married.

When we understand clearly what our goal is, then it becomes much easier to decide if what we are doing will help us reach our goal or not. If what we are doing is not bringing us towards our outcome, then we can gladly change our strategy for something more empowering without the hindrance of tying it exclusively to our identity.

One of the most powerful things to notice is that people tend to link identity with achievements or goals in a way that may not be fair or accurate. Many people will come to know others by what they have done in the past, and sometimes we judge ourselves now by the mistakes we have made or our accomplishments. Some people have experienced the relative who always knows us by some stupid thing we did years ago. They don't seem to be able to want to get beyond it, and they tie it in some way with our identity. It is to be hoped that we've also had the relative who identified more with our potential, who knew we would be something great or something special. Holding a believable identity based on a future goal can be very empowering.

We want to remain aware of the impact we're having, because this can backfire too. Sometimes the well-intentioned family member can promote the idea of achievement to the point where the child feels overwhelming pressure to be a certain way, to set goals outside of their comfort zone. If the child does not feel they can access an adequate sounding board to reach that goal, they may feel the expectation is unfair, that they are being pushed.

The truth is, we are more than our past, present, or future. These are not us; they are not our total identity. Others may tend to link these things with our identity. That does give us an opportunity to raise our personal standards and set achievable goals in line with our standards, thereby favorably tying our identity to positive things. It is important to remember, though, that we are doing this as an empowering choice/tool, using the same principle that allows people to feel bad about things they have done, turning that around and empowering ourselves to reach elevated goals.

By setting a large goal, you are making a commitment towards your future identity. If you're getting married, your identity will be that of a wife or husband. That is a new and powerful role for you; you'll need to start to think differently, and your identity will change. Just becoming engaged is a big step. Now you are a fian- cée; this is a new identity and you are operating toward a new set of goals. People recognize your identity as different and they treat you differently.

These sorts of identity shifts can be a little bit strange because they reorient our thinking process. Sometimes we do not like this reorientation and we stop pursuing that goal. Other times we may like the idea of a goal because it does reorient it the way we think; we like the idea of having the identity that is linked with that out- come. Some people will select a goal for that reason, and they never make a serious attempt at achieving it. They just want to be seen as someone with that identity and they want to operate from that perspective, with that sounding board. Have you known anyone who has talked and talked about doing something but they never take the steps necessary to achieve it? Does the goal elevate their sense of identity?

A powerful thing to remember is that when we lock our own identity or the identity of someone else with the past, it may not only be unfair, it also could be difficult to change that perception. On the other hand, if we link their identity with those things they're committed to achieve, then we are reinforcing the positive intent and confirming their ability to change. We may be adding the validating support that will really assist them.

Chapter 13

That's Right — Validation

Validation serves an essential part of our thinking process. It is just as important to the process as goals or anything else. The reason is simple:

- Our evaluation process consists of asking and answering questions as the basis for decisions that lead to action.
- For the process to end, we must be able to determine whether our answers are correct.

Validating Ourselves

First of all, we need to be able to validate ourselves as we journey through the endless asking and answering/evaluation process that is our life. We would not be able to function if we could not trust our own ability to correctly answer our own questions. After all, if you can't trust yourself, who can you trust?

In our evaluation process, we ask ourselves questions relative to some outcome or goal, and we need to evaluate the answer we receive. We either decide that something is true or false, or that we should do something, or that we should not do something. Sometimes, of course, the answer will be "I don't know." If that is the case, hopefully we will move on to another question: Is this important? How can I find out? Somebody else may step in here and try to help us. But we still need to decide for ourselves whether the helpful person's information is accurate or not. Nobody can do that for us.

Validating Others

With others, validation or affirmation is the process of complimenting somebody or agreeing with them and making them right. It is saying that they are doing the right thing and that their feelings and actions are appropriate and appreciated in some way.

On a deeper level, it is acceptance and communication of worthiness as an important member in the relationship. The relationship could be a working environment, some sort of team or family situation, or any situation with two or more people. The smallest gesture could be received as validation. You could compliment someone's dress as you stand in line at the store, and they could feel validated because all the decisions they made about acquiring and deciding to wear the dress are receiving some external corroboration.

In cases where someone has very little self-confidence or belief in their own ability, we can still see this to be true. A person may lack all confidence in their ability to be decisive. In reality this might not be true of them at all. Here's an example:

Patient: Doctor, I'm not really sure why I came here. I guess it's because I don't have any confidence at all. I can't take a strong position on anything or believe in my own ability to be decisive.

Doctor: That's the silliest thing I've ever heard. I think you're making the whole thing up.

Patient: That's not true! What kind of doctor are you? This is my problem. I've had it for years. I think I know much better than you do exactly what my problem is. Don't tell me that you know better and I'm making this up.

Doctor: I apologize if I offended you. I'd like to change your mind though. How confident are you in that position?

Patient: I'm not falling for any of your tricks. I'm 100% confident that nothing you say can change my mind.

Even if our thoughts are irrational and all over the map, we still have a need to trust our own judgment!

When someone feels validated, they may also experience a feeling that they are understood: someone finally understands who they are and why they do the things they do. We all operate from the premise that we are making good choices and decisions, and when someone else "gets that" about us, we appreciate it; we like to know that our assumption that "we are doing the right thing" is correct.

Active Listening Is Validation

Crisis and suicide counselors get extensive training, and active listening skills are considered to be the most essential tools. Would-be counselors who fail to properly implement active listening or appreciate its necessity will not be forwarded on to work with people. Of course, active listening *is* validation. Crisis counselors listen and agree and try to understand the reasoning that got the person into their crisis. No negative judgments are allowed—only curiosity, interest, and indications of understanding or requests for clarification on the way to understanding. All of these responses are forms of validation. By actively listening without judging or trying to come up with solutions, counselors help people feel understood. Empathy and validation of the person's emotions as understandable responses to their situation really helps people feel better. The person is thereby enabled to come up with their own solutions.

Active listening is particularly helpful for people who like a great deal of feedback from others. It helps the person to feel confident that at least their reasoning skills are working okay and they can feel that their experience is normal. Feelings of normality for a person in a problem situation are very important. The person may fear that being abnormal will lead to rejection from others. Criticism, contempt, avoidance—all are the opposite of validation. Such responses from others all signify that you have been judged and found deficient in some way. (Remember, being judged and rejected is our biggest emotional fear.)

Validation Can Be a Matter of Life or Death

Following the Columbine school shootings and similar incidents, schools have identified and implemented policies to protect children from experiencing criticism, rejection, or other physical and emotional bullying. School authorities have recognized the potentially tragic consequences of kids being bullied. We have learned from these calamities how strong the need is for validation. When kids are labeled as being weird, different, gay, stupid, or just "not the kind of person to be included in our good feelings and activities," they can have very strong emotional reactions. The reaction and its intensity will depend on how many needs the child is trying to satisfy in the school context, as well as how they satisfy their needs and how important the context is to them.

For teenagers, the context of their peers generally is the most important one. It is where they are looking to establish or learn how to establish loving relationships as adults outside of their immediate family. Therefore, what the other kids think and do and who they approve of is magnified.

Because the need for validation is so strong, kids who are left out as social outcasts may tend to group together so that they can validate the experiences they are having with each other. Some who may be a bit different, but not exactly outcasts, will be motivated just by the fear of rejection to conform and act in the way they believe their chosen group would appreciate and validate. When you act like others ones, you validate them, and you get a reinforcing group relationship.

Validation Can Save Relationships

We do seem to understand that people need to feel validated in their lives. It would be great if we always just freely validated what we like in each other. Often though, this is not the case—people are far more likely to use a critical approach in close relationships, where we have the closest encounters with people's behavior and are especially likely to believe some of those behaviors should change. Many couples who started out all googly-eyed and finding every little thing about their partner interesting, fun, and sexy, end up turning a critical eye on every fault or inadequacy of the partner, even exaggerating the imperfections that they would like the partner to notice and correct.

Dr. John Gottman, researcher, therapist, and professor, tells (in his charming way), in his certification trainings for marital counselors, how couples tend to perceive the counseling experience. Typically each partner has a story of how the other partner is broken, and please fix them! On top of that, each begs for validation of what a kind and loving person they are, one who is willing to deal with such a difficult, imperfect partner and under such difficult circumstances. They may humbly admit that they are not easiest person to live with either, but their own imperfections are cute, charming, and unique.

The therapist's challenge is to help them both to realize the part they are playing in the relationship trouble, without devaluating either of them. A neat trick! Of course, not all therapists understand this. Many people quit couples counseling. Usually it's because one person felt the therapist was not on their side and was blaming them and validating or otherwise siding with the partner. People do not stay with a therapist who cannot recognize or validate their good intentions. A good therapist will validate the highest intention of both members of the relationship. When couples can agree on their best intentions for the relationship as being things like love, commitment, and family, then they can work on specifics to achieve them.

Unfortunately, not all of us have competent, trained therapists knowledgeable about validation and ready and willing to act on or intervene for our behalf in our delicate social communication. People without training in validation typically try to influence each other with negativity. They yell, they complain, and of course they threaten and withhold love and validation. This kind of devalidation will only work with some people who, for some reason, either want to comply with you or have to comply. If they have to comply, they are not likely to validate your methods. With kids, even though they are getting some benefit from complying with a negative directive, if they feel the approach is unjustifiably critical of them, then the problem of communication will become more of a focus than whatever issue the parent was trying to work on.

Grandparents Are Great Validators

It seems to take some of us a lifetime to learn the lessons of validation. Many grandparents seem to have figured out that you get more bees with honey than vinegar. They spend time with the grandchildren, they listen to them, they tell them they are right, they ask them questions, they show genuine interest and care (even if they weren't so great with their own kids). They accept and love the grandkids unconditionally.

Although the approach of the grandparents may not be the best overall approach for the parents to take in raising the children, it does help us to see that such an abundance of validation can help someone to develop and appreciate a good self-image as well as have confidence in themselves and their ability to have positive relationships with others. It also shows that once our need for validation is met at a high level, our natural response is to express positive emotions or love. After all, do we not remember our loving grandparents with love?

Validation and Identity

When we were young and we were being taught the ideas of right and wrong, it was likely taught on the level of identity. The big people hardly ever said this to us: "Your evaluation process is not giving you the correct answer, which is likely a result of some reasoning that made sense but was not necessarily true." No, we are told, "You are wrong." We hear this as a statement about our identity as a person—we take it very personally. When we are told that we are making a mistake, we get that we are being judged as an imperfect being. This is very hard to shake. Even if you re-performed the task brilliantly, your identity keeps the "wrong" label.

It doesn't take too many uncomfortable experiences before we begin to put a very high value on being right, or at least being seen as being right. Possibly even more disturbing than that, we learn to value not being seen as wrong. When a teacher asks a question and requests a show of hands, many kids won't raise their hand until they are absolutely sure of the answer. The higher value can be, not having their peer group see them as wrong.

Inner vs. Outer Validation

Just as with the introvert/extrovert scale in the Myers-Briggs test, we can notice a pattern with need for inner versus external validation. (This scale pattern holds true for all the needs, by the way.)

Some of us prefer other people to tell us we are right, preferring the approval of others to our own. In extreme cases, such a person may selectively lack the inner ability to decide if what they're doing is right. This type of person will always be asking others what they think and will still have trouble making their own decisions without that assurance.

Midway in the range are people who like external feedback, but once they have it, they weigh the information and decide for themselves the appropriateness of their decisions. This is, of course, a place of balance, where people have a good sense of themselves but value others opinions as well.

Further up the scale are those who have a strong inner compass. They will be much more selective of which feedback they take in, and they will "consider the source" as well as notice the motivations of the information provider. They will be strong in their convictions and direction, but will gladly accept what they consider to be quality advice or feedback.

At the high end, of course, are those who are rigid and strong in their opinion and have no need for anyone else's opinion or feedback. They already have it all figured out and consider more information a threat, as it could pollute their pure way of thinking.

It is good to remember that the internal and external feedback ratio that someone prefers will be contextual. The headstrong teenager who is very closed to the idea of feedback in the context of their conduct in the family system may be very open to feedback or advice from others in areas they believe will satisfy their needs. For example, the teenager may be happy to listen all day long to someone talk about good and bad tattoos and tattoo artists.

That's Right, Validation

Lastly, the title of this chapter," That's Right, Validation," is a nod to Milton Erickson, M.D. (1901-1980). Erickson incorporated hypnotism into therapy sessions at a time when doing so nearly cost him his medical credentials. His results, however, were so outstanding that other clinicians in the 1950s agreed that there was need for a distinction between hypnotic parlor tricks and the genuinely effective use of hypnotism for medical and therapeutic purposes. Since that time, Erickson himself has been held up as a model of excellence in hypnotism.

One of his most amazing talents was his ability to simultaneously have a conscious conversation with a person and hold a different conversation outside of the person's conscious awareness. In the conversation outside the client's awareness, he would address difficult issues.

He was also able to induce altered awareness: trances or hypnotic states. Over the years he filled a notebook with hundreds, perhaps thousands, of language patterns that he had used to assist people to enter a trance state. He began to test and remove all but the most effective patterns, and he went from a full notebook, to three quarters, then to half, and finally just a few pages, with the words evaporating like rain on a sidewalk after the sun comes out. He tirelessly tested and removed and tested and removed. At the end of it all, he had only two words left, two words just as helpful at assisting someone into trance as all the other patterns that he had so painstakingly learned and refined over the years. Those two words were, of course, "That's right."

As Erickson would sit with a client, he would comment on little things the client did, saying, "That's right, I see you have decided to sit in the more comfortable chair," or "That's right, you saw on the desk the cookies that my wife made." As the client did things that were going in the direction of a trance state, he would say things like, "That's right, your eyes want to close." They would relax, and he would say "That's right, you are ready to relax even more." Part of going into a trance state is being relaxed, which of course happens when a person is comfortable. These two words seem to work like magic in getting people to relax; they build trust and comfort.

I offer you what I think is a very valuable suggestion. If you speak these words at the right time, you can satisfy a person's need for validation and need for a strategy simultaneously. These words say, "Don't worry, what you're doing is fine. You are enough just the way you are." Since the target for verification that our strategy is good exists outside of our awareness, these two validating words will have an emotional impact on us. The feelings would be similar to the feelings when another need is satisfied, such as certainty, significance, or love.

So, that's right. You guessed it. Catch people doing things that are good and tell them, "That's right!"

Chapter 14

Certainty or Survival

In Western cultures it has long been accepted that the first law of nature is self-preservation. To act instinctively on our own behalf for the preservation of our life is recognized as normal, healthy behavior. The only situation in which we are clearly justified in taking the life of another is to defend ourselves from someone attempting to take ours (self-defense). Generally speaking, the view is that if a person does not act in the preservation of their life, there is something wrong with them and they are not functioning properly. The only exception is in cases where one puts the life of another ahead of one's own. Even in those cases, the person is acknowledged for their ability to override the natural instinct to protect themselves to serve a higher level idea. Because of our need to survive, certainty at times will be valued by all of us at high levels. We need to be in a safe environment. If we are not, then we must take action until threats are minimized.

With "certainty," we see the need for physical survival, where we must stay alive and feed and clothe ourselves, where we can find adequate food and shelter and reasonably defend our physical selves. This dovetails into a more emotional target where we want stability in our relationships, our sense of identity/strategy, and our ability to satisfy the rest of our needs.

If we hear that our company may be sold or that a large number of key people will be laid off, our need for certainty will be ignited. It is natural for us to experience several different emotions at a time like this and for us to consider and decide upon the best course of action for ourselves. By deciding on a best course of action and having contingency plans for different outcomes, we will regain a level of certainty. How good or how strong we feel will reflect the confidence/certainty we have in our alternatives.

We need to feel a basic level of certainty in our lives to behave "normally," i.e. "appropriately."

Let's have fun. How important is certainty, really?

Imagine it's 7 a.m. Picture your upcoming day: Think of all the people, places, and activities you will interact with until bedtime. Got it? Good. Now let's pretend that you just heard on the news that there's only a 2% chance that the sun will come up tomorrow. Only a 2% chance that life as you know it will continue. How does your day feel now? Would it be the same old-same old? Or something else entirely?

Relax. This was just an exercise, and the sun will most likely come up tomorrow.

My intention was not to scare you, and I do have a point, which is that it is very difficult for us to carry on normally if there are threats to our need for certainty in areas that affect us physically or that affect us on an emotional level.

Certainty in Relationships

Many top marital therapists understand this. Therefore, they try to teach their battling couples the key principle, "Do not threaten the relationship." Threatening the relationship by attempting to coerce the partner into some behavior rarely has any beneficial effect and often causes damage to the relationship that may not be easily repaired. It's like saying, "The sun will not come up tomorrow". This hits directly at many of our needs, including the need for certainty. How can we carry on normally if there's a great deal of uncertainty if the relationship will continue? Crazy as it sounds, after a while, leaving the relationship starts to seem like a comforting alternative: At least there will be some *certainty* as to what is happening, and planning will become possible again.

The need for certainty is stronger for some people. Some of us are very concerned with safety and long-term planning. We tend not to like extreme challenges or things that take us away from routine. Many people will select their life partner based on filling their need for certainty. They will select someone who they feel to be safe or someone who can provide financial stability or is certain to be a contributing partner, placing this even higher than their need for love or a deep understanding or connection. (Of course other people would like those safety-providing qualities too. I'm talking about *priority*.) These relationships are called "marriages of convenience." While deep love can develop from these unions, that is probably the exception, due to the way the relationship invalidates the partners. Unfortunately, this type of marriage may be appealing for some people who feel too vulnerable to express feelings of love. This of course can lead to unnecessary feelings of isolation and suffering for both partners.

Certainty at Work

Cloe Madanes states that we need to be certain that we can maintain relationships with other people, at least at a workable level or a standard we are comfortable with. We need to have a sustainable and reasonably positive relationship with our employer and co-workers. If we do not, we will most certainly be unhappy.

Certainty and Children

Of course what has just been said deserves even more attention when we are dealing with children. Adults have some sense of independence and control. They can, if they have to, make alternative plans for housing and other needs. Children, on the other hand, are totally dependent on adults for their physical safety as well as an emotional environment of stability and certainty. Children are much more likely to take our statements literally. If we make a statement such as "It's all over," the child may be too immature to understand the boundaries or the context of the statement. Words we throw out in a fight with our spouse may hit our children at the level of survival, even though they were only exaggerations for effect in the heat of the moment

Intellectual Certainty

As we move down the spectrum from physical well-being to *feelings* of certainty, we see that we require, just as intensely, certainty in the way we use our own brain. We need to feel certain that we are evaluating things and making decisions correctly. Are we being rational or irrational? Here is where things get really tricky! Stereotypes come into play and keep us from recognizing the universal truth about how we make decisions. Women are seen as better at using emotions or feelings or even some sort of intuition in their decision-making process. Men, on the other hand, are credited with using hard facts and logical data. Both of these gender-based stereotypes are just wrong! Ultimately, *everybody* confirms decisions with *feelings*.

Try this out for yourself. $16 + 16 = 32$. Right?

How do you know? Do you have a *feeling* that it is 32? Did you think, "This is the right answer" and back up those facts with a feeling of certainty and conviction? Of course you did! There is no other way. Not sure? Go back and do it again. Trying to only use thought and no emotions or feelings. You can't do it.

The need to *feel* certain of your answer to this simple question is exactly the same need you have when you answer all your life questions as you make plans for every aspect of your life.

No matter what the question, we need to *feel* that our inner representations of the outer world are correct and that it is safe to act on them. Put as simply and primally as possible, we need to be able to distinguish between a piece of rope on the ground and a snake.

The need for certainty pervades every aspect of life, physical and intellectual. We need a feeling of certainty that we can maintain continuity in our external environment to satisfy our physical needs. Yet we also need certainty about our strategy, the feeling of certainty that our feelings, opinions, or decisions are right and will help us to satisfy our needs. Everyone will attempt to satisfy needs for certainty on these two levels.

The need for certainty operates on one of the widest ranges of any of our needs: It extends from the basic needs necessary for survival that we share with all other forms of life, to the needs of social interaction, and up to how and why we think and make decisions the way we do. Ultimately they all come back to this question: How certain do we *feel*?

Chapter 15

Variety, the Difference That Makes the Difference

Variety is an emotional need! To live in a world where each day is the same and everything looks the same would certainly drive us mad. This fact about us is as basic as our five senses, which are designed to identify discontinuities and differences and immediately notify our conscious mind.

The wind blowing on our face is different from the stillness just before. When the tone of someone's voice changes, it indicates danger or concern, or playfulness, or love, or just that dinner is ready. If we see a sinkhole in the road that wasn't there yesterday, we make adjustments. When we see something new, we have to compare it with things we do know something about, sort it all out, and continue from there. Realize we are all different in how much difference has to happen before we see it as a difference.

Regardless of these differences, for our happiness, we all require *some* stimulation, novelty, or surprise. In fact, the whole premise that makes comedy funny is the mixing together of things in unpredictable ways that create joyful surprise.

Variety in Intimate Relationships

Here, boredom can be the killer. When we become too accustomed to each other and we go through the same routine year after year, we can experience a certain amount of unpleasantness that we may unfairly blame our partner for. How can we let this happen? Well, it's not anyone's fault. It's just that our need for variety is not as life-and-death important as our need for certainty or survival. Because of this, we may reinforce certainty so much that we stop taking chances and create an environment that doesn't value variety in a healthy way. Who knew?

Marital therapists generally agree that couples should regularly engage in activities that help them to experience variety. They give various advice, such as having a date night where just the two of you go out and experience some new things together to keep the relationship fresh and unpredictable—anything from skydiving to dressing up to go out to a new, fancy restaurant. Maybe you just need a great vacation! Whatever works.

The Need for Variety Isn't Always the Same Throughout Life

The degree to which we value variety seems to change throughout our lives in a somewhat predictable way. Malcolm Gladwell pointed out his book *The Tipping Point* that small children experience variety or difference almost constantly, mainly because to them everything is new and different. Because of this they seem to appreciate similarity or sameness quite a bit. They want stability in the family structure, and they tend to believe that things are permanent and will always be a certain way. Because of this, little kids can watch a TV show or a movie repeatedly, each time being excited about and reveling in their knowledge of what will happen next. For little ones, the predictability is very fun and empowering. This is eventually replaced by a drive to experience things that are exciting because they are new and different. It changes again when people start having children of their own and safety and certainty again become important.

Many people stay this way, but some of us experience a midlife crisis in which we remember that life used to be about variety and excitement. This can work out well if the methods we choose are appropriate. We are all familiar with the 45-year-old gent who trashes a perfectly good marriage, only to crash and burn (sometimes literally) speeding down the freeway in a new sports car.

So How Do We Satisfy Our Need for Variety in a Good Way?

Two ways.

One, externally, through socializing, travel, hobbies, television, the Internet. This option, of course, does most of the work for us.

Two, by ourselves, with our own imagination and creativity. When we start to believe we have nothing more to learn, our excitement about life drains away. One antidote Robbins promotes is curiosity, opening our minds to discovery. A nice side effect of cultivating curiosity is that when you become curious about another person, they are likely to feel validated. Do your kids, your spouse, or your parents feel as though you are genuinely curious about or interested in them?

Here's a thought! How about being curious about yourself? How many ways can you be more, better? Even if you are physically limited in some way, self-improvement is possible: physical, mental, social, spiritual. You might even get healthier and smarter. There's evidence that people who keep their minds active with puzzles, games, music, and the like retain more cognitive ability. You can always build new neural pathways (mental muscles).

Caution: Do not confuse variety with mere distraction. Distractive activities are those that typically satisfy only our need for certainty, that is, a sense of certainty that there is always somewhere we can go to take us out of the boring rut of our everyday lives. Examples of purely distractive activities are eating, video games, TV, and Internet surfing. By definition, distractions are the opposite of intentional focus (positive or otherwise). They may not be immediately harmful, but they usually have no meaningful goal or outcome. We don't have to be intensively goal driven every single second of life. That is not even healthy or sustainable. There is nothing wrong with and experts agree occasional mindless relaxation is essential. The trick, I think, is to find ways of satisfying your need for variety that also inspire you and motivate you to take action on your life purpose and goals. I think you already know what those are. This is just a little reminder.

Chapter 16

Significance, Self-Esteem

We all share a desire to feel significant, important, unique, or special. The variety of ways people have found to satisfy their needs for significance is astounding. Our ideas about what makes someone significant are formed in our environment at an early age. We also picked up on cultural cues. Many of us try to fill this need by making gobs of money or knowing more about a subject than anyone else. Any public contest entertainingly testifies to this compelling human need.

The need for significance can, to some extent, be traced to and recognized in our participation in nature's mate selection process. Survival of the fittest is based on who can reproduce the best. Many animals spend a great deal of their time and resources developing means by which they can demonstrate their superiority in abilities to protect the group and offspring, or build shelter, or demonstrate physical strength and beauty or dexterity. All are designed to gain favor of the opposite sex and pass on the DNA.

People are no different from non-human animals in the courting process. Other social systems are involved too. We like to be recognized as successful at work, socially or in hobbies, in whatever strategy we are committed to, with the ultimate goal of feeling significant and favorably connected with others.

Many woman value and express self confidence as the highest desired trait in a male. Any man's core strategy for attracting a feminine women will be enhanced when he learns the important differences between confidence–self-esteem and significance driven arrogance.

Chapter 17

Contribution, Belonging to Something Bigger

Presence is Your Gift

Being present in the now has been long held as an elevated way of experiencing this magical experience we call life. Many popular ideas have been sought out over the ages teaching to how to find the power of the now or the power of the self. At some point, all of us wish to feel that our lives meant something and that we mattered. Feelings of disconnection and worthlessness seem to be the opposite of what people desire.

Contribution is what the doctor ordered, for many reasons. Number one, disconnection is a state of mind. For whatever reason, we may believe it better to be uninvolved or disconnected. This is the opposite of the truth. Feeling disconnected is nothing more than a really bad way to associate to the very things you are emotionally connected to. Acknowledging our connectedness and participating in that relationship by contributing brings you immediately into a heightened state of presence.

Number two, contribution is acceptance of your environment. It does not mean that you are saying everything is perfect. It is saying that you have a realistic view of the world and you feel empowered to participate and confident you can make a difference. This is quite the opposite from attempting to withdraw and not participate in life.

Reason number three is maybe something you haven't considered before about contribution. It speaks of allowing yourself deep involvement in life. This *something* I like to call "ownership by interest." What I mean is, if you are interested in something and pursue it, the world will make way for you and acknowledge your ownership in that area. Let me give you a couple of examples. Henry Ford was interested in the manufacture and sale of automobiles. No one authorized him to pursue this life direction. Purely by being interested, he became the undisputed leader in that area. Same with Thomas Edison. With practically no formal education beyond the third grade and armed only with an ownership interest in those things he pursued did he (like Ford) forge ahead with untold contributions to humankind.

This universal pattern or truth can be seen repeatedly. People like Gandhi, Mother Teresa, Shakespeare, Galileo, Newton, Aristotle, were all elevated to their station in life and history not so much by the sanctions of others but almost solely by the ownership interest that they applied in their fields. Investing ourselves with genuine interest in meaningful contribution may be a risk-free way of not only making our lives more rewarding, but also of living a life that matters.

The fact is, you are now in this life with this world to experience it in. It is your choice to participate with care and ownership. . . or not.

Chapter 18

Love and Connection with Others

We all need to experience the feeling of love or at least connection: with others, or God, or nature.

It serves us very well to notice and remember that this need— and all the other needs—really represent an emotion or an emotional state. They are targets that we try to experience through our interactions with our environment.

Love is nearly always understood as the highest and most positive of emotions. It is an emotion that we experience as individuals, yet also share with others. We can experience the emotion of love towards other people or our environment, our Creator, or even in relation to life itself.

The experience of love can be described as a *feeling of positive connection*. Even though we don't fully understand why it is so important, we have seen instances where the emotion of love seems absolutely necessary for life itself. Science has shown that human babies who are left alone for long periods of time without loving, nurturing physical stimulation will die. We now know that our physical well-being is very much connected with our emotional state. Patient attitude, and the very real placebo effect of inert drugs, are well documented as important factors in patient recovery.

We don't grow out of this, or any, need. Strong statistics support the idea that we require loving connections throughout our life with people and things, or face some very negative consequences. For instance, some credible statistics indicate that once a man hits retirement, he has a fairly good chance of being dead within 18 months of his retirement party. The workplace may have played a major role in satisfying needs for love-connection-belonging (as well as, of course, other needs, such as significance, contribution, certainty, strategy).

For both men and women, various independent research gives evidence that failed marriages are linked with reduced life expectancies. Dr. John Gottman has shown that intimate relationships that contain negative emotions such as contempt are related to increased illness and decreased life spans.

As we learned earlier, people have different ways of experiencing feelings based on the meanings they ascribe to situations. For instance, some people experience the feeling of love all the time and believe it to be a natural response to the world, whereas others rarely, if ever do, believing that feeling love makes then vulnerable in some way, or that there are only certain conditions when it is okay to feel or express love.

What Are Feelings? Are We Safer Avoiding Love?

When we have a feeling about something, we may recognize that it is not necessarily true. We could have a feeling that a salesperson or someone is trying to deceive us when they are not, or some other feeling that may not be substantiated. That's one kind of feeling. There is another more important one that is of a different nature. Having the feeling that our life has no meaning, that we are separate and we have no positive connection with anything, may be very harmful to us. The amount of time and the intensity with which we experience that emotion may directly affect our health and our actual lifespan. The quality and length of your life maybe directly related to the positive emotions you experience with your environment as perceived by you.

Historically there has been confusion on the part emotions play in our lives. Science has been unable to locate, identify or even describe in a comprehensive useful way what emotions are in the human body. We call them feelings, but they are different from things we feel by touch or with our other physical senses. We do feel our emotions, that is for certain, yet it is different from feeling a tangible object.

We cannot accurately measure our emotional ability with an external source. That is to say that we cannot say that Mrs. Smith has more of a certain emotion than Mrs. Jones. No one has proven that there's any discernible skill or ability that can be linked with whether or not we experience emotions. It seems like common sense that we are all born with a natural ability to experience a broad emotional range. How much of those emotions we regularly experience seem to be a matter of conditioning. We all have emotions that we experience over and over on a continual basis, and if we chart them out over a week or a month, we will find that we run a small pattern of a few emotions over and over.

Some of these emotions will be positive, and some will be negative. We may justify these emotions by our prior knowledge that it is proper to feel a certain way in a certain circumstance, yet we must remember these feelings are not the same kind of feelings we get when we touch a table. These emotional feelings are generated by the meaning we have associated with some person or circumstance. When two people touch a table, they can agree on the feeling it generates. It feels cold, hard, smooth, rich. Yet when two people are introduced to a new situation or a new person, it is much less likely that they will have the same emotional feeling. Much disagreement in our lives with other people is based on not being able to appreciate or agree upon the proper emotional feelings to our life experiences. We believe our feelings about someone or something are accurate, are justified. Other people have different feelings and of course believe they are equally justified. And of course they are.

The point here is that we all have a broad, capable emotional range, and still we tend to only experience a small percentage of our emotions on a regular basis. Besides that, there are emotions some of us tend to only rarely experience, while others experience them all the time. This does not seem to have as much to do with hereditary or environmental conditions as with the meaning people associate with those emotions. For instance, some people experience the feeling of love all the time and believe it to be a natural response to the world, whereas other people may believe that experiencing love makes them vulnerable in some way, or that there are only certain conditions when it is okay to feel or express love.

Same with depression. For some people it is easy to feel the emotions of sadness or depression, believing them to be the appropriate feelings in relation to the world around them. Others may associate feelings of depression with suicide or some sort of weakness. They may believe those emotions are way too painful and take drastic steps to avoid them.

Our willingness to experience emotions hinges a great deal on the deeper meaning we place on the emotion. For this reason, we can expect an ability to improve our emotional life with the proper map, and the desire to use it.

Emotions are critical for us, as they operate as a type of communication that is much quicker than language and can take direct control over our nervous system. In fact, verbal language is fairly new for us as a species, and we lived a long time before we had formalized language skills. In all likelihood, when humans were in a pre-language era, we judged the meaning of each other's grunts and yelps by the emotional intonations placed upon them. We see this now in the communication of animals. A dog who is emotionally excited or fearful will put those emotions into their voice tone as well as in their physiology. They will effectively send a message. An animal who is defending itself will send a clear emotional message that it will attack if you do not back down.

Emotions may very well be a type of communication that can be understood more universally than previously thought. It may extend to communication between species and from communication with our Creator, all the way down to communication on a cellular level. After all, is there not a profound emotional vibration associated with love, prayer or meditation?

Some of the benefits of emotions are most easily seen in the emotions of fear or emotions that make us respond to danger. Having a fear of large carnivorous animals or a healthy fear of heights has allowed the continuation of our species. Such fear seems a natural response to the environment and takes control of our nervous system, putting us in what the psychologists term "fight or flight mode." Psychology has long held that there are only two things in our physical environment that everyone is born being afraid of: loud noises and heights. If this is true, it means, of course, that all other fears are learned. We have to learn what to be afraid of; we must make some association between things that for us generate the emotional feeling of fear. This explains why different people are afraid of different things. Someone may be excited about holding a new gun, and someone else maybe terrified to even be in the same room with it. This shows that emotions can be manipulated to a point where they can be as intense or greater than our instinctual or natural fears. As well, people can learn to be excited and happy about jumping out of an airplane or being in a loud environment like a concert, reversing the intensity of our natural emotional reaction to external things.

Different meaning, different emotion. This shows how meaning is more important than the actual physical circumstance in our emotional process. This is important, because many people feel as though they cannot control their emotions, and they believe they will always be at the emotional mercy of things that happen around or to them. The truth is, the facts just do not support those beliefs.

Consider areas of your life where you do not feel you can experience love, and ask yourself, "What changeable meaning prevents me from feeling love in this area?" Or better stated, "What can I now believe or remember in relation to this person or situation in order to feel a deep love?"

Chapter 19

The Need for Growth

The need for growth, like the need for contribution, is an important and valid need, even though neither may be required for our survival in the same way as, say, love and connection. Tony Robbins also makes this distinction and calls them "the needs of the spirit."

A good example is the fact that even in the strictest of incarceration settings, isolation (preventing connection) is less likely to be used as long-term punishment because it is understood that isolation is unusually cruel and can lead to mental breakdowns. Yet in the same settings, withholding the ability for the prisoner to grow and contribute does not constitute quite as cruel a punishment. That being said, any confinement with hope of rehabilitation of the prisoner does recognize how essential it is to draw out and honor an individual's desire and ability to grow and contribute.

Though we can technically survive when the emotional target of growth is not met, it still has a large effect on how we view ourselves and our world, and is related to our health and mental well being.

We all go through stages, pivotal points in our lives through which we learn and grow into a larger perspective; typically, baby to toddler to preschool to school, and on to college, followed by career, courtship, marriage and family, empty nest, midlife, grandparenting, retirement, perhaps partner loss, and then a stage where we prepare for our own death. All of these stages build upon the preceding stage and are necessary. If we don't grow to the next stage, we can get stuck and may have trouble or miss opportunities that naturally empower us to satisfy our needs. For more information on life stages, I recommend the book *Uncommon Therapy*, by Jay Haley.

Growth has a bearing on our intimate relationships. Psychologists usually recommend separation when the relationship is abusive, and there is another area where many also recommend separation: When one partner feels he or she has outgrown the other, it is often viewed as an irreconcilable difference.

In one sense, of course, all life is growth; each day brings new knowledge and experience. The kind we are talking about here is the result of the *intentional* desire to gain knowledge or to stretch ourselves beyond our previous understanding or limits. It's finding an emotional target in the results of curiosity, the desire to learn. If it is true that something is either growing or dying, then could it also be true that growth, and the emotional payoff, is essential for us to be healthy on a level of cellular emotional communication? Maybe it's another sad fact, like babies dying when they are not loved.

It is no secret that people feel more fulfilled when they're excited about new opportunities or they feel they have broken through some previous obstacle. Even people who typically do not like a great deal of change or the idea of growth experience a feeling of exhilaration or higher self-value when they have been put in an environment that requires them to really apply themselves and grow.

Increasing the level at which we and those close to us satisfy our needs produces sustainable, fulfilling growth.

In the previous section of this book, we described what the needs are, why they are important, and how we can identify them. We want to remember that everyone must regularly meet all of these needs and will attempt to do so, even if they have no conscious awareness of it. However, once we are aware of the process of need satisfaction, how well any of us perceives that we are satisfying our needs can be measured. If we use the Robbins scale of 0 to 10, zero would be used for a need never being met, and 10 for it being regularly met at a high level. It is helpful to identify the different areas in our lives, such as our most important relationships, activities, or identities, and then rate how well we are satisfying our needs in those contexts or categories.

We may regularly satisfy several of our needs at high levels through work or some other activity and fail to satisfy our needs at high levels in our intimate relationship or our family, or vice versa. Because of our desire for validation, we may focus more attention in the area where our most valued needs are being met and less attention is other areas. By simply rating ourselves in our areas of importance, we can understand how to bring more growth and balance in our lives with the use of the needs.

Just having an awareness of how well you are satisfying your needs, and then doing even small steps towards positively satisfying your needs, your life will improve immediately. By understanding the needs as unconscious targets that we will move toward, we are empowered. Without that awareness, we have only a vague sense of what our emotional targets are and what it is we should be doing to reach those targets. Because we were trying to reach those targets in the past, we have developed a strategy that we believe is appropriate for us given our particular conditions.

Take a moment and consider how you satisfy your needs for growth. Chances are you do many things, and the ones you really enjoy probably satisfy several needs. Maybe some of them could also satisfy your need for growth. Chances are also that these really enjoyable things are satisfying your sense of identity and purpose. Maybe you hate your job—it doesn't come anywhere near satisfying your needs for growth. It seems like a miserable dead end. Still there is something you can do. Perhaps you can decide to learn more about different aspects of your job, such as how it affects other people. This may be very effective if one of your top needs is connection with other people. Ask yourself, How can I satisfy my top needs in this job? You can always seek out opportunities to delve deeper into certain skill areas, for example, and you can always study to gain expertise. There's always room for meaningful change and growth. Knowing the targets helps with direction and vehicles.

Chapter 20

Strategies, Not Stubbornness or Ego

Everyone, consciously or not, is running a strategy they have developed and that they believe is the appropriate way to behave in relation to themselves, others, and their environment. So when we see somebody behaving in any particular way, we can know that unconsciously they believe what they are doing should satisfy some or all of their top needs.

They are revealing their strategy in their actions.

People believe and feel at their core that what they are doing is right, and that if there were a better way to act, behave, or feel, they would have noticed it and made the appropriate adjustments themselves. If you, as an outsider, question their behavior or offer better solutions, you will likely be dismissed as not understanding the overall perfection of that person's strategy. Because a person's strategy is so unconscious and invested in the person's judgment and experiences, any criticism is generally taken at a highly personal level. The person may not feel that you are questioning what they are doing, but rather you are judging them on the level of identity. You could be accidentally telling them they are wrong as a person. To be effective in helping anyone, including ourselves, we must separate "the way we are satisfying our needs" from "who we are as a person."

I did not come by this understanding easily. While doing many different kinds of research in human behavior, including years of helping people on crisis and suicide phone lines, I realized there were some interesting commonalities in people. For one thing, I noticed that when a person was feeling bad and admitting their life was not working, they still believed in and condoned what they were doing. They were desperately clinging to their beliefs, even if they felt suicide was the most reasonable option. While they might listen to someone else's opinion how their situation could be improved or looked at differently, there was a level of conviction where a persons reasoning could not be penetrated unless their beliefs were validated or sided with. When you think about it rationally though, it's ridiculous to even consider as a possibility that ending one's life is a good idea. The thing that made me a believer in strategies as a need was that no matter how desperate someone was, everybody was always willing to perk up and give advice to me about their own strategy and how I should become more like them. Odd perhaps but when I inquired, everyone happily gave me their recommendations. This reveals the existence of a level where we all validate ourselves as making the best choices and responses given the situation.

Before this experience of talking to thousands of people in emotional and situational difficulty, I (and most people, for that matter) may have labeled this sort of behavior as defensive, stubborn, irrational, or egocentric. Instead, I now saw a universal pattern. A pattern so simple that, once it is recognized for what it is, will greatly assist someone with a desire to change. It is quite different from the idea of ego. Although similar to ego, it is also a pattern so strong that it will allow the person to approve of behavior that is destructive or even fatal to the self or others.

The key to unlocking this pattern, when it is destructive, it is to understand that it is a pattern of choices someone is making to satisfying their needs. When we understand what needs they are trying to satisfy, we can find behavior and vehicles that serve everyone involved better. This is true of a repeated pattern of self-destructive behavior or an isolated incident where someone is truly desperate, having lost their inner belief that they have a strategy to satisfy their needs that works in their current environment.

The reason we haven't seen through to this pattern before may be largely due to looking at individuals as though they were their behavior, or that their behavior reflected some undefined part of themselves such as their ego or unconscious. I think it's time we asked, "Do these old ideas lead us away from clear thinking that gives us solutions?" Do terms like irrational, stubborn, egomaniac, actually prevent us from thinking of solutions?

As part of a behavior model for explaining unconscious processes, Freud introduced the *id, ego, and superego*. It is well accepted that this model was perhaps good theory that did not translate into good practice. The initial definitions of these terms have changed over time, and today the ego is more understood as someone's self-esteem or an exaggerated sense of self-worth, and in some cases is linked with our sense of identity.

Creating the term ego may have been fine if the theory had stopped there. Unfortunately, speculation by some clinicians and the general public did not stop there; many went on to assume a connection that egocentric behavior comes from some permanent physical part of us called the *ego*. This is a stretch of reason that sounds good because it identifies a cause. So good, that it was accepted as practical. This, even though we are usually using the term to define a behavior, there is no part of the human anatomy called the "ego." Logically we know reasoning based on the existence of something that does not exist may obstruct clear reasoning and should be reconsidered.

To describe how someone is behaving or acting as being influenced by their ego causing them to be an egomaniac is not reflected in practical reality. To suggest there is a part of the human anatomy called an ego and another part that must keep it in check is to falsely create a map of nonexistent attributes. When this is done on a physical or identity level, it accidentally presupposes that change must also be made on those levels, rather than in behavior or our inaccurate maps.

I think Freud probably had the right intent though. Whether it's ego or strategy, we are talking about a model for changeable behavior. In this case, I am clarifying and describing the behavior more accurately as a "process." It is not an attribute of any individual; it is only our best unconscious effort to satisfy our needs.

Consider the following simple problem as an example of attribute misuse. Someone who does not know something can be taught it, right? At least usually. Whereas, if we say the very same person is "a dumb person," we might consider that person to be incapable of learning. (It's their identity.) In the first case we know how to handle a situation. In the second case we are not empowered to take the correct action.

We may believe that we cannot be fooled by these things and that we would somehow know the difference between someone lacking information and someone who is incapable of holding or processing information. In our fast and frivolous lifestyles, those little distinctions of how we categorize people shape our lives more than we may realize. What about others? What if we tell a four-year-old that they are a dumb person? Just to make sense of what you had said, they will need to make a map or picture of themselves with "dumb" as an identity-level trait.

This cannot be helpful.

I believe the term ego can be done away with in these contexts once it is recognized that what we're really trying to describe is the strong emotionalized conviction with which we unconsciously value our strategies. By simply understanding correctly that we are talking about a very changeable process rather than an unchangeable attribute, we are redirected in a way that is helpful and empowers us to unlock the mystery.

Just to clarify, I am not saying that ego and strategy are the same thing. I'm saying, in my experience, that all we need to understand is strategy. When we do, there is no need for the term ego, freeing us from its unintentional obstructions and unhelpful negative bias.

Chapter 21

A Snapshot of How and Why Strategies Develop

Just to review, by strategy I mean a person's behavior pattern, conscious and unconscious, that the person believes should satisfy some or all the other top needs.

Our strategies develop at an early age. They are conditioned patterns of behavior that have become associated with need satisfaction. They may be things that directly get our desired results for us, or they could be something we just happened to have been doing when good things came to us. Either way, strategy patterns are hooked up with needs being met, and so our unconscious says, Yeah, I liked that. Good strategy! Keep it up! For instance, a baby will learn that when it cries, people respond with milk, attention, or a diaper change. Psychologists now teach parents to respond to their children by satisfying needs when they exhibit positive, desired behavior. When doing something (even something like giggling) gets such a great result, it can easily become a lifelong pattern. What a world it would be if everyone giggled when they needed something! Unfortunately, even if a strategy is destructive to oneself or others, it will continue if enough of the needs are being satisfied at high levels.

Learning to Play the Needs Game

We begin learning as toddlers that other people believe certain things are more important than others. If we learn to accept the big people's values, very often at least some of our needs will be met. (Of course, if we reject their values, that indicates that we are meeting other needs by doing so). For example, if Big Sis is satisfying her need for love and connection and significance through being an outgoing Little Miss Sunshine, we may get even more significance and genuine concern for our well-being from the parents by rejecting their values and being a little hellion. We may even outdo Big Sis with number of needs met. This is a common pattern in families and can cause much unnecessary heartache.

Strategies Evolve along with Our Peer Groups

The shift from childhood to puberty marks a change in how, where, and with whom we associate satisfying needs, from the original nuclear family to other important structures such as friendships, love interests, and the person's relationship to the larger society. Strategies can shift then, because adults and children satisfy their needs differently. Values may unconsciously become more aligned with a peer group as we search for acceptance outside the nuclear family. Teenagers for generations have commonly rejected the strategies and values of their parents in favor of seemingly ridiculous peer-approved behavior. If teenagers are not accepted by the majority because they don't have the right clothes, or aren't smart enough, or too poor, they may instead join a counterculture that also satisfies their needs—they fit in by being different, such as becoming a computer nerd. Usually not a problem—but there are glaring exceptions. For teens, the need to have a strategy that works is so strong that rejection from the larger peer group can lead to suicide or even worse, such as the Columbine tragedy. The truth is that the Columbine shooters believed their strategy was good, but for some reason it was not working. They were no longer able to satisfy their needs regularly; they were outcasts and made to feel insignificant by their peers. By coming back to school with weapons, taking charge and hurting people, they were at least able to satisfy their need for significance at a high level and punish those who failed to validate them. They felt they were running out of choices in dealing with their environment and that the only way to be certain they would satisfy their needs would be to take the actions they did. If only they been empowered to change their strategy! Though their goal was incredibly negative, it nevertheless allowed them to immediately satisfy their need for significance at a very high level. And they did! Even today people are discussing them. Their need for connection too—they formed their own group and gave each other lots and lots of validation. They even connected in a profound way with their victims, the school, and the community.

People generally tend to dress and act according to the group or class of people they would like to be a part of. We make snap judgments constantly about people we see, about their honesty, industriousness, social inclusion, and we decide if we would like to be around them. Unconsciously we are evaluating if these people are helpful or dangerous; we can predict to some degree how they are satisfying their needs. If they are satisfying them in ways that are harmful, we will get a sense of that and choose accordingly.

These patterns may seem like more of a problem than they really are, in most cases. For one thing, it is an opportunity to practice behaviors for mate selection. After a few years these outlandish behaviors lose their charm, and we turn back to the values of our parents and the larger society. We are validated by whatever peer group is our current one. This is why so many people eventually do turn into their parents.

Strategies Change When Needs Focus Changes

The need for variety is a good example, because this a high need for most young people, always on the lookout for the latest craze, for excitement. In a few years, family life, house, and career will cause a shift toward a high value on stability and certainty. Twenty-somethings may prefer jobs with lots of travel, while family types look for health insurance and minimal risk. Retirement may again bring the urge for variety, travel, and new experiences. Adjusting needs in this way is a sign of a healthy outlook that is in touch with a broader picture of what is going on in one's life.

Relationship challenges often stem from failure to adjust or align needs. Women tend to recognize the sense of responsibility that is required to raise children and place this need above variety. Men will often try to satisfy all their needs without giving up variety. Finding ways in which everyone's needs are met in positive ways that support everyone is key to long-term happiness.

Environment Influences Our Need Satisfaction Strategy

Many children who were raised in the 1930s learned to value certainty at a high level. Depression-era people are or were likely to have extra money tucked away and value paying off their home mortgage and other ways to reduce any financial risk.

Many successful people have a very high need for significance and/or certainty, and often have been successful in spite of coming from impoverished circumstances where they felt insignificant and uncertain. It is a common belief that if we have enough money we could travel and experience variety, plenty of friends, and could court that special somebody who is currently out of our league. With enough money, others will validate us because we're so cool; we can pursue meaningful goals and contribute in a way that will make us feel alive versus making it to the end of the week.

It might even be that the need for significance, such as status in social, employment, or financial terms, stems from our need for mate selection and reproduction, to stand out in a unique way through strength, stamina, or beauty. The winner of such a contest passes on his or her genes and lives a purposeful life, and the loser does not.

To summarize, the strategies we use to satisfy our needs relate to those things that we have come to believe (because of our conditioning) are the best ways for us to do so. There are a few problems here: strategies may be based on things that are no longer true. They are based on associated feelings (inaccurate sounding boards), not necessarily conscious thought. We cannot wish strategies away. When we wish to change our behavior, we may find it difficult to change with conscious thought alone. To insure permanent change in our lives, it helps to consciously reconsider our emotions using intense positive associations to appropriate vehicle related sounding boards and outcomes for the current stage of life.

Chapter 22

Our Strategies for Love & Intimate Relationships

From birth on, we develop strategies for satisfying our needs based primarily on what we feel overall is possible or works. These strategies affect our personalities and behavior because of our tendency to form generalizations over how we need to be or act.

Moving the Strategy Out Into the World

Forming generalizations is very normal, but it can cause problems when they are not updated for the various stages of our lives. Let's consider, for example, a child who is continually reinforced with positive emotions from his or her parents and others for being helpful and cute and perhaps respectful of others. The young person will decide that is the way they should be, so they may start acting cute, respectful, and helpful in nearly every situation as they move out into the world: school, work, with friends. They may begin to feel these traits are *part of their identity* and become known to themselves and others as a cute, helpful, and respectful person.

This strategy of being this person has worked beautifully within the family context. It is easy to understand why this behavior will move into different contexts. It is highly valued behavior, most of the time. But not always; sometimes it may not be appropriate, may not be supported, and can even get the person into trouble.

Let's say our cute, helpful respectful person has grown up to be a 33-year-old married man with two kids. He loves his wife and wants to be helpful and please her in a respectful way, but for some reason his strategy, which by all accounts is positive, well thought out, well intentioned and sanctioned by society, has stopped working, and his relationship is in trouble. His wife hates the way he is because she thinks that the man's role is to be a decisive leader who guides the family in a positive way. She doesn't like being the decisive one, and fails to appreciate how much he is trying to operate in a supportive role to her needs.

In his mind he has failed at being helpful, being respectful only makes it worse, and it's hard to be cute when nothing you do works. Like many in such a situation, he turns to friends and family to validate him. When they tell him what a great guy he is, he is likely to keep thinking that he should just keep on being himself: cute, helpful, and respectful, It is easy for him to conclude that his wife is an unappreciative scold and there isn't anything he can do—somehow she needs to be fixed.

With that decision, an error has been made that will need correcting before things will get better. When we view ourselves as being at the effect of circumstance or others, we stop looking for ways to adjust our behavior internally to get the outcome we really want.
He will have to recognize that his behavior is only a way he has been using for quite a long time to satisfy his needs. He will need to understand that his strategy of being cute, helpful, and respectful can be easily changed. He must understand that this is not who he really is, and that he does have a choice about how to behave in his own family, a way that is different from what he learned as a child. He does have an opportunity to have a much more successful and fulfilled life, whether his wife changes her behavior or not.

We all have our strategies for dealing with intimate relationships, from avoidance, to very skilled and effective love and seduction techniques. Our example above was probably oversimplified; most people have a fairly extensive repertoire of behavior that has worked well and continues to do so, yet they will still run into relationship situations where they are less than effective. We all use different strategies to satisfy our needs, and we value our needs at different intensities. Theoretically we will all come across some issues because the number of combinations created when you put two different people together can be astronomical. Fortunately, most people tend to operate in a smaller range and satisfy their needs in similar ways, and the breakdowns tend to be similar. Dr. Gottman points out that a realistic view is to expect any time two people are together, there will be at least one thing that is unresolvable, and the relationship should be cherished anyway.

The Nuclear Family as a Source of Need Satisfaction

As we grow, it's normal to move from our immediate family for need satisfaction over to friends, hobbies, and love interests. The timing of this transition is based to some extent on how well the nine emotional needs are being met. Children who are not well served by their nuclear family will become dependent on non-family members for need satisfaction at an earlier age. Conversely, we've all seen in strongly bonded families who share activities, care for one another, and have worthwhile goals that the kids tend to do well in school, create lasting friendships, attend and graduate college, and avoid the rebellious, disconnected stage. Having all of their needs met at high levels fosters a sense of abundance, which enables them to feel good about helping others satisfy needs, among many worthwhile outcomes. These kinds of outcomes have little to do with economic resources, as long as survival needs are being met. We are talking about the parents being available physically and mentally in a supportive way. Perhaps families in the developed world may even find that an emphasis on financial achievement can get in the way of satisfying emotional needs. Financially comfortable families who succeed may be doing so in spite of their economic environment rather than because of it.

Intimate Relationships Need Focus

No matter how well a strategy is working for the kids in a success-ful families to satisfy their needs, if the family remains the primary source of need satisfaction when the person moves into an intimate relationship, there will be problems. If either adult partner is not allowed to assume their proper primary role in need satisfaction, the relationship will not be very fulfilling.

Personal friendships can also be a problem for intimate relation-ships. After moving out of the family system, we move into a sys-tem of friends where we are significant, validated, find certainty and variety, and know our strategy is appreciated. When we move into an intimate relationship, jealousies can occur there as competi-tion develops over who is now going to be the source of need satis-faction. Associations with coworkers and work team members can create similar conflicts. Young workers often satisfy all their needs through their career, especially when employees are expected to put in long hours, or when there are expectations that the work en-vironment will also be a social environment.

We always attempt to find ways to satisfy our needs and hit our emotional targets, even if our intimate relationship somehow is not doing it for us. Let's say we do not feel important in our relation-ship. We will look to our job, or sports, or hobbies, or friends, or having children, or even our parents, as fallback. The needs are so strong that, if unmet, people will violate their own standards to sat-isfy them. Under certain circumstances, a person who places a high value on being faithful will nevertheless "go astray." Let's say your strategy is just not working with your partner: they are critical of you and invalidate you at every opportunity. You feel unhappy and insignificant. You may begin to punish your partner by deliberately not satisfying their needs, in hopes they will "wake up" and do their part to satisfy yours. Hurt and resentment will likely build up, and soon you might find someone at work who does listen to you, who does see your many sterling qualities and talents, who vali-dates your strategy on a daily basis. Who wouldn't prefer to be around the person who makes you feel successful (unlike the one at home who makes you feel like a failure every time you are together)?

Even if your partner successfully helps you satisfy most of your needs, if they are not satisfying the ones most valued, you could be sorely tempted. You may seek another relationship. If not that, you will still desire satisfaction. You will find some other vehicle to directly satisfy the need, or you may unconsciously find yourself seeking distraction or doing something to bring attention to the problem. If you can punish, shock, scare, or make your partner jealous in the bargain, so much the better. Most of us have experienced or witnessed this sort of situation.

Guys, Woman Need Us To Grow Up

The shift from satisfying our needs in our nuclear family to satisfying them as an adult in various contexts, especially through intimate relationships, is an important step in human development. Males in Western society still have some important lessons to learn to succeed in high levels in intimate relationships. In other words, the strategies we use to give and receive love and attention from our mothers are the same ones that will make our girlfriend or wife want to hit us over the head with a frying pan. We must consider the context! If we do not, our strategy will be the problem or the real reason we are not satisfying their needs. Young men need not be apprehensive about relationships. They merely need to take a long look at their role as an intimate partner. It is easily and naturally fixed, once understood.

Intimate Relationships Are Not Essential

None of this is to say that you need to start an intimate relationship or have a family environment to satisfy your needs. It is a problem when a person would like to have one, or sees themselves as moving to the relationship or family stage, as part of their identity. It can also cause stress for a person if they place a poor meaning on not having a relationship and believe it reflects poorly on themselves from the perspective of people they care about or the greater society.

There are two stages of life in which people are more likely to commit suicide than at any other times. They are the stages of becoming senior citizens and the stages of young adulthood (in that order). From a strategy standpoint this make sense, because these two major transition periods require a larger shift in the strategies we use to satisfy our needs than any other life stages. Not only that, but the stakes are raised as to the consequences for not making the shift in the way that empowers us to satisfy our needs in the new life stage.

If we move into adulthood or our senior years continually failing at our attempts to feel important or significant, and we feel we cannot create meaningful emotional connections with the people we desire to, and it seems our best efforts and intentions are not validated by society, we may feel that it is hopeless or pointless to continue and consider suicide as an alternative. For every person who commits suicide, there are countless more who carry on experiencing some sort of emotional misery, wishing there were something they could do.

Remember that there are unlimited vehicles and ways to satisfy your needs, and not everyone is interested in having an intimate relationship or starting a family. That is perfectly okay, just make sure the needs are satisfied in healthy ways.

Chapter 23

Role Models as Shortcuts

So how do we get this transition into a good strategy? While some people move effortlessly into various relationships with an ease and intuitive sense about what they're doing, most of us do not. We make mistakes, fail, fumble our way through, and try to figure things out._We ask friends and learn by trial and error. However, there are shortcuts that anyone can use to understand what they need to do and make the transition. One of the biggest shortcuts is no secret, yet its importance is not often taught or explained in the right way. It is the idea of *role models*. It is so helpful to appreciate how a role model can aid in the learning of complex human behavior in a way and with a speed that other learning methods have trouble competing with.

The copying of roles and behaviors is a trait that we share with many other creatures in nature. We may have an instinctual learning process associated with role models that can speed up learning Role models can also be a great aid to us in our decision-making processes. What would Uncle Henry do? What would Gandhi or Jesus do? Using role models in this way provides us access to our own powerful internal resources that have only been touched upon by psychology. We are very fortunate in that our role models do not need to be related to us, have similar backgrounds, or even be close to us in geography or time. Through such resources as history books or biographies, videos, and the Internet, we can now access role models for nearly any endeavor we wish.

Although elementary, roles can easily be overlooked, and it is definitely worthwhile to look at the various roles that we have in our lives and really ask ourselves if they are right or if they need updating. For example, as parents we need to constantly update our role so that we are not treating our 39-year-old son as though he is seven years old. To make a good transition from satisfying our needs in a family situation to satisfying them in other environments, we need to recognize that our role in the new relationship is different. The role of boyfriend or girlfriend is different from the role of friend. The behaviors need to be different in relation to how we satisfy our nine needs; the role has to be updated. When your intimate partner complains about you with a statement such as "You're just too immature for me," they are in a sense saying you don't match their idea of a role model as a partner. That is not to say that they are necessarily right and you should change. It *is* saying that understanding roles in relationships can help us greatly in quickly identifying needed or desired behavior, especially when you consider that in an intimate relationship, the roles become stacked. In other words, you are expected to have many roles: best friend, lover, partner, companion, trusted advisor, taxi driver to the airport at 3:30 in the morning.

By understanding roles, you can make easy transitions in all areas of your life to optimize what you are doing for your best outcome. Taking on roles isn't always a piece of cake. Sometimes people take on roles or responsibilities but fail to take the time to understand what is required of those roles, or they believe the new role will somehow have a negative affect them. As a common example from the workplace, many people who are excellent workers get promoted to a position that requires more skill and understanding than their previous position. Many times this happens without proper training or full employee understanding of the new role. In other words, people can be advanced beyond their competency. If they see the promotion as no more than a reward and do not really update their old role, they will likely fail. If they understand the need for a fresh perspective and flexibility (possibly finding a role model to emulate) they are much more likely to succeed.

In intimate relationships, it is extremely valuable to find out your partner's expectations of the roles you are to perform. It is also equally important for you to clarify the roles you need to have fulfilled by an intimate partner, taking full responsibility for the role definition and approaching it this way: "Honey, I love everything about you and feel I can trust you so much that I feel I can open up and express that I need for you sometimes to_____ (fill in the blank). If you could do that to help me with this silly thing, it would mean the world to me." Besides knowing the roles, you want make a list of those roles that would ruin a relationship for you. Men have roles that they do not want from their partner: the nag, the cheat, the clinging vine. Likewise women have roles they do not want from their partner: the mama's boy who wants her to be his mama, the man married to his work. By making a list, you can notice before you get in a relationship if there are roles that are mutually supportive—or not. If you're in a relationship, you can compare the roles you like and the roles you dislike. By understanding that your partner is turned off by some particular role you thought was cute, you may be able to adjust your behavior so that they really do think you're cute.

Role descriptions are nothing to take to personally; they are only roles, behavioral shortcuts, models for you to use in the appropriate settings. A lawyer might be excellent at interrogating a witness on the stand and bringing truth to justice, yet this role needs to be left at work, because not too many families will appreciate the woman's lawyering when she comes home and starts interrogating the family about why dinner isn't started yet.

You can still be yourself when you are filling a role or using a role model. It is impossible not to be yourself. Always realize that you are good enough, and you want your strengths and personality to be fully alive. Role models are just shortcuts for mastering tasks and aligning expectations between people. It's very much like learning to draw using tracing paper. You practice with the image you would like to duplicate fully available for you to copy, and then, as you become more comfortable with practice, you can draw by yourself and still refer to your mental image. In the same way, you hold ideal role models in relationships, business, family, health, religion, school. How much happier would you be with your life if you committed to making that image your standard of operation in those categories?

You also have a perception of an ideal partner. Many wise people have asked, "Who would you need to be to attract such a person and live the life together that you would want?" The image you come up with will provide you with your own internal role model. Is that who you are now, or do you do need to make some adjustments?

We know how important role models are for kids at various stages of their development. This value does not fall away just because we are grown up. Because of just how available and effective role models are for us to succeed at different complex behaviors, I wonder if we should be purposefully using the best ones we can find to assure our success in areas where we might not have thought to use them before.

Chapter 24

Our Most Important External Relationships

When we talk about roles or strategies, we are also defining our relationships with other people and the rules for appropriate or praiseworthy behavior. Part of defining and understanding these different roles and strategies is understanding which relationships are more important than others and why. If we were to go out on the street and ask people what their most important relationships are, we would quickly hear such answers as . . .

- Children
- Parents
- Intimate partner
- Important friend or mentor
- God or a religion

If we ask them if this is always been true for them, we will usually find either it has, or there have been only a couple of changes in their whole lifetime.

People experience a myriad of challenges because of the relationships they value most. Generally, we tend to place a high value on the people and relationships that we perceive as helping us to satisfy our needs.

Please take note: Valuing those relationships solely based on the satisfying of needs can throw our whole lives out of whack. This is true because, if we place a high importance on a need-satisfying relationship over and above our most important role and purpose, our other relationships can suffer. A few examples:

· The intimate partner who values spending time with buddies over and above the intimate relationship.
· The intimate partner who values the need-satisfying relationship with one or both parents (for various reasons) more than the one with their partner.
· The husband who allows his mother to butt in and tell his wife how to best handle the household.
· A partner who satisfies needs mainly through the children, or worse yet, children from a previous relationship.

Favoritism has the potential to cause trouble anywhere three or more people are interacting. In the work environment, nepotism and favoritism create relationships that are not consistent with normal business structure, and if not addressed, the relationships that have been unjustly subordinated will suffer. Whether it's employees looking to stand out from each other with the employer, or siblings vying for the love, attention, and approval of the parents, there will be problems if the leader fails to clarify his or her role and relationship with everyone involved.

So the answer to the question, "Is there any most important external relationship?" is yes—and no. For a healthy person, the most important relationships should change over time with the person's life stage and circumstances. We need to also recognize that maintaining important relationships should not create conflict. When we were born, our most important relationships were with our parents, family, or those whose care we were placed in. From there we were presented with many relationship choices: grandparents, siblings, teachers, friends. When we reach adulthood and start our own family, it is natural and healthy for our primary focus in relationships to change to our spouse and children. In our senior years, it is natural for people to value first their relationships with family, followed by those with friends.

Part of understanding roles is to understand the expectations of which needs should be met by those relationships. For children, all of their needs should be met at high levels by their parents and immediate family; it would be unusual for someone else, such as a neighbor, to be in the first position of helping the kids to satisfy their needs. For a married couple, this post should be for satisfying needs at high levels for one another. If these needs are being met largely by a friend or coworker and not the spouse, the relationship could be weakened.

We all have expectations of how we would like others to behave in their relationships with us, and every person's expectations and definitions are different. Roles help us to form agreement on those expectations, and we can even improve upon that when we layer in a deeper understanding of the nine needs and how they should be met in our different relationships.

Challenges arise when people value satisfying their needs higher than respecting the roles and relationships they are involved with. Anyone who has cheated on their partner certainly has placed the satisfying of their own needs above the relationship. By understanding how our needs can and should be met in our various relationships, we can move from feeling as though nothing is working for us and possibly never will, to having absolute control over how we can be fulfilled. What is perhaps even more important, we can help others to experience inner fulfillment.

Chapter 25

Everything in Our Environment Serves Us

Whatever our environment, we will use it to attempt to satisfy our needs.

If we take all of our experiences in a single day and divide them into two categories, we can gain some valuable insight.

1. Things that we believe are favorable.

2. Things that we believe are unfavorable.

How you choose to sort your life experiences will be a great determiner of the quality of your life. For now, I will ask only, how do we respond to things that we call unfavorable?

I ask this question because everyone, including me, is running a strategy. We are deciding on appropriate behavior to handle any given situation based on our unconscious belief that this is how we should be able to satisfy our needs. People respond to challenges in their own unique way. Some are overwhelmed by a challenge and seek sympathy or loving connection. Others embrace challenge as an opportunity to gain significance by showing others how well they handle adversity, and possibly gain loving connection as well. Some of us cycle between strategies. We are all unconsciously trying to satisfy the same needs, even though our approaches differ widely. However, and this where it gets interesting, our unconscious is <u>not</u> necessarily interested in satisfying our needs in only positive ways.

So when we are presented with an unfavorable situation in our day-to-day life, if our needs are met at high levels by categorizing things as unfortunate and out of our control, we may self-validate this decision. We must understand that although externally we want a positive outcome, our ultimate response to the situation is based on satisfying internal needs. If calling our situation unfortunate satisfies the needs, we will accept the negative external environment label.

The decision whether we should feel that we are *not* resourceful enough to handle a bad situation, or the decision to feel that we *are* resourceful enough to handle it, may be more a matter of satisfying our needs than having the skill to handle the situation. This explains why some unemployed people feel justified in making statements that explain their behavior, such as "I can't get a job. It's impossible to get downtown. Nobody will ever want to hire me." By deciding to represent things in this way, the person may not have a job, but they do have what's more important, a vehicle that they believe will satisfy their needs.

If you were to ask me which needs someone doing this is satisfying, I would have to say it would depend on the person, and add that it definitely seems like a pattern heavily linked with the core strategy; they say they do it because it's "who they are."

We may also know people who intentionally choose to sort things as though they are challenges so that they can constantly look like a hero as they solve the problem. "It was tough putting that light bulb in, but I did it. I'm so significant." These people tend to be cheerful.

A bully may be trying to satisfy a need for significance as well as certainty that they can get a response and perhaps some variety, even if the response is punishment and being intensely disliked. So to them, it may feel rewarding to behave in this way. (The bully usually sees himself as a good person who's lashing back at the world and its people who have not validated what a great person they are and strategy they use.) Violence and bullying are a strong indicator that the individual is having trouble in satisfying their own needs in some area of their life, likely in the area of a key relationship.

Certainly our environment also provides positive opportunities to satisfy our needs. A career in contribution is a good example. A teacher may teach to feel significant and confirm with certainty that others will benefit from what is being taught. It could even be some variety and personal validation. So to them it may feel rewarding to behave this way.

There is no shortage of ways to satisfy our needs. The truth is that, if anything, there are way too many choices. What becomes important are the criteria for selecting vehicles. If we select based only on speed and convenience, with no consideration given to the overall affect on others or ourselves, our overall emotional health will suffer.

Our environment will serve us and our needs. We should remember and idea of how our mind works from Earl Nightingale, "The soil in our garden does not care what types of seeds we plant".

Chapter 26

We Believe Our Behavior Will Satisfy Our Needs

We probably don't think about our behavior in these terms, but no matter what we do, constructive or destructive, it is a reflection of an inner belief that says that behavior will satisfy one or more of our needs.

When we understand which needs a person is trying to satisfy, it is much easier to understand, connect, and develop a more meaningful relationship with them, be they a friend, coworker, client, family member, or anyone, really. The same understanding applies to ourselves. By understanding our own needs, we can know how to best satisfy them and have significantly better life experiences.

The quickest and best way to find out what needs people are satisfying with their behavior is fairly straightforward: ask them. We see what they're doing, we start to get a sense of why they're doing it, and then, when we ask them, we can be pretty accurate.

If we do only the first step (seeing the behavior), there's a good chance we will be wrong, for a couple of reasons. One is that different people do the same behaviors for different reasons. One person may run for president to satisfy their need for significance at a high level, and someone else may run for president to contribute to others and honor their parents' belief in them. If we just take a wild guess, we might be completely off base and inadvertently project our own motivations instead.

On the other hand, sometimes our guess is pretty accurate. Many behaviors are good vehicles for satisfying certain needs, and it is appropriate to generalize about them. For instance, much animated behavior can be seen as an attempt to satisfy the need of significance. Such behavior could be described as loud and jovial, or even signifying emotional distress or potential violence. In any case, people nearby such behavior do not have much choice about being involved in the extreme behavior and grant the person some sort of significance, whether they want to or not. People can also become loud and extreme while they are trying to satisfy their need for certainty. For example, if a person becomes very upset because of a threat to a relationship or job, facing a situation with perceived or potential loss and resultant uncertainty, they will be loud, They will be using this behavior as a significant force to get clarity—the certainty they need in relation to whatever it is that they are upset about. If you have a hunch that certainty is the person's top need, you may want to act on that and give it to them. If you do not, they will continue the behavior until they do satisfy that need, change their focus, or come to understand a better way to satisfy it. In the past this behavior may have served to get results. Therefore, it now seems natural to them, and they think it is a good idea.

We know the truth in this. We have all seen situations where people satisfy needs at high levels in destructive or counterproductive ways. How does this happen? For many people there is a threshold point, a "last straw," when they believe they have tried their best to satisfy their needs in positive ways, and yet it didn't work, and perhaps gave them pain. Sometimes we think we have done all the right things and given it our best, and yet our lovers leave us, or people criticize, reject, or invalidate us (while, of course, reinforcing/validating their own strategy or values). This happens to everybody when we mistakenly jump to the conclusion that the rejection or devalidation is a reflection of a permanent condition outside of our control. We then may begin to satisfy our needs negatively. (This is a key to understand and correct violent behavior.) We may not understand why the behavior that ends in despair is in some way also causing us to feel better.

These methods of feeling better typically take a very short-term view of our overall life and situation. Harmful addictive behavior is always a short-term view of how to satisfy the needs, whether it is drugs, smoking, violence, or overeating, and is used where a long-term strategy is clearly needed. Some of these destructive patterns come as a strategy of failure—consistently satisfying needs by failing. For some people it seems nothing can go right, regardless of the fact that others in their peer group are doing fine; they keep missing the strongly desired target that would give them fulfillment.

Closely related to that is the strategy of not having any goals. This can show up in several ways. One is lowering expectations for life and not really setting any emotionally desired outcomes that could lead to disappointment. Another is not setting goals as a way of punishing those who care about you, especially the people who care if you succeed. There are ways to justify such behavior: maybe to punish one's parents for failing to satisfy childhood needs. Yet another is to use the challenges that inevitably result from not setting goals as a springboard for need satisfaction through commiseration sessions.

We must, therefore, be very aware of our own strategy and check it to make sure that it is based more on the reality that life is an ongoing process and direct it towards our larger, positive goals. If we have a strategy based on short-term comforts while disregarding the larger context of our lives, it is predictable we will overindulge in things like food, drugs, or attempts to nurture ourselves with negative emotions such as self-pity.

Chapter 27

Fear Good, Faith Bad

This is a good time to bring up an almost universal experience so that we can notice it and learn about the best way to turn it into a positive advantage in our lives.

It's *fear*. What I'm talking about is based on the idea that it is preferable to experience fear verses faith. Logically we all "know" we would prefer to be in a positive state with positive expectations, yet we go through our day-to-day lives conditioned to value our ability to recognize danger. This too makes sense, because if we do not recognize danger, nature's process of elimination will eventually wipe us out.

How often each day do you recognize opportunities for faith in a positive outcome? Perhaps an odd question, but bear with me, because there is a point. Chances are you do not have a radar (sensory awareness) that alerts you to opportunities to enter a state of faith in the same way you have a radar that senses danger and causes you to experience a state of fear.

Because of this fear radar, there is a perception, and rightly so, that our guard should be lowered to allow us to experience fear. We rightly value recognizing danger. On the other hand, the hand of faith, we tend to become conditioned to the belief that allowing ourselves to operate with the emotion of faith may lead to pain. For example, we have trusted someone to provide or do something, and that person lets us down. We soon become suspicious of being in a state of faith, and raise our guard, making it harder to go into that state. Also, it's easy to fear what others will think if we decide to have faith without being able to give others any tangible reason for having it. Having faith could threaten our basic needs, because others may reject us on some level for being a silly fool.

Remember, though, that one of our top needs is the need for certainty. It is important that we are able to go into a state where we can operate as though there is certainty in our environment, some predictability, where we will find definition that validates our decisions and actions. How do we get certainty? By having faith! How do we reconcile this paradox? The way that most of us resolve it is to place faith in our fears.

We need to operate as though the sun will come up tomorrow. This shows the way we generate a state of certainty by using faith. However, there is no requirement that we need to believe tomorrow will be a good day. We could just as well have faith that it will be a bad day. It may make emotional sense to authorize ourselves to go into a state of worry or fear about what will happen tomorrow. After all, we are benefited by recognizing danger, and others will possibly commiserate with us if our future looks dark and threatening. So we can have faith that things will *not* get better, that we have no control, others are heartless and do not appreciate or understand us. Is this the best strategy?

Here is the reason I say this is a timely topic for this part of the book: We want to have an excellent strategy. An excellent strategy has to contain the ability for us to encourage our own state of faith based on *positive* expectancy. We can and should understand danger and appreciate our nervous system's ability to warn us of danger with the use of fear. We should also notice that that skill is probably overdeveloped, and realize it is okay if we stop focusing on it and trust that our unconscious will always respond appropriately to danger. Overindulging in *fear-based faith* (negative expectancy) is a strategy that will satisfy many needs and can become addictive. However, it is based on short-term gratification and is imbalanced, in part because the encouraged emotional states are mostly negative.

Willfully authorizing ourselves to experience "positive expectancy" as a way of experiencing certainty in our future is a prerequisite for an excellent strategy. There are negative expectancy weeds in your garden! Pull them and give them no further consideration. Instead, focus your attention on the seeds you have planted, the abundance of life in the garden and your relationship to it, and your faith that the seeds you sow can produce only the plant from they were derived.

Positive expectancy will empower you to take action towards your desires in a way that defines you and others positively. When you are empowered and taking action in the direction of your desires, you are more likely to experience what you desire than if you had not even tried with a fear-based faith. Not to mention that life is a process, and to experience it with positive expectancy is to allow yourself an immediate luxury that so many inadvertently decline. When we learn to satisfy all of our needs through living a life of positive expectancy, we are likely to experience a highly beneficial sense of fulfillment or oneness.

We talked about having *certainty* through positive expectations. What about the other needs? We can also have *variety* by allowing ourselves to pursue the things we desire in external achievement and in deepening our relationships with others. It is better to be validated for being a positive leader (if only for yourself) than it is to be validated and pitied as someone who expects the worst in life. Why not take the bull by the horns and make it all one hell of a ride?

As for *significance*, who do you believe is more significant, someone who is a positive force for good for all, living life on their terms, deciding to have faith until it pays off even when the environment doesn't support it, or someone who wants to be significant by complaining loudest, or putting others down, or parading in front of others sad tales of the enormous life challenges that have brutally beaten them down? Positive expectancy to *love* is interesting, because realistically we can experience the emotion of love, joy, or any euphoric positive state any time we want, for absolutely no particular reason.

So what holds us back? Negative expectancy? Is there a fear that if we open up as positive loving euphoric beings, the result will be pain? I hope I have shown you how we may have come to unconsciously believe this is true. Moreover, hopefully I have shown you that employing a strategy that validates opening up our unlimited wellspring of positive emotions is a better way to go. By doing so we connect with ourselves and others in a much more positive way, encouraging personal growth and contributing directly and indirectly to the lives of others. To satisfy all the needs, you would want to use the NLP (neurolinguistic programming) guidelines for ecology: make sure your goals are good for yourself, good for others, and serve the greater good.

Chapter 28

We Are Not Good at Satisfying Our Needs

For the most part, people are not good at satisfying their needs. We *believe* our behavior brings us in some sort of *general direction* that we *hope* will help us experience the things we value most. We try many different things.

- We act in ways that we learned as children would get approval from others, or at least attention.
- We adopt the values of people around us, either to be successful like they are, or be seen in a favorable way by them.
- We adopt role models and take on the behaviors of different roles, all the while expecting that there will be a payoff in our environment and ultimately we will achieve emotional success.

Both conformists and nonconformists have trouble satisfying needs. Whether we actively invest ourselves in mainstream ideas by participating in the system, going to school, building a career, and being a productive member of society, or we opt for individualism and nonconformity, thereby aligning ourselves with a non-mainstream group, the intent is the same. That intent is, of course, to satisfy our emotional needs. In either case, most people fail to do that. At one time or another in our lives, in almost all contexts, we can expect difficulty in satisfying our needs.

On the one hand, it is common to see someone doing all the right things and still being miserable. They have good health and education, they have upper-bracket income, are good people and are generally well-liked, yet some parts of their lives are a nightmare. It could be their career, children, or their intimate relationship, but there is some area that is keeping them from success and fulfillment. High-status roles and identities may be a good framework and shortcut for us; however, they do not work all that well without an understanding of our targets.

On the other hand, we do need people who challenge conformity and promote individuality. They serve an important function, and are rightly accepted and encouraged by many people.
People serving in this role, however, also meet with failure in many areas of their personal life—career, health, family. By being someone who challenges the thoughts of others, they may experience more trouble in interpersonal relationships or getting others to combine resources to solve some of the problems that define their cause.

In either case, it can be heartbreaking to see people with the best of intentions, who really care about people and have put themselves out there, taking a position of strength and really feeling justified that they have done the right thing, yet failing to have the oyster of happiness open for them. When things don't work out in certain ways, or their relationships fall apart, they can easily experience the feeling that they are not understood and loved at the level they should be.

For us to be successful and good at satisfying our needs, we need to expand our understanding of the targets we are really after. We know in our hearts that simple formulas like "Money can't buy you love" or "Early to bed, early to rise, makes one healthy, wealthy, and wise" may hold a deeper wisdom, but they certainly do not provide all the insight we need.

A big shortcoming of roles and identities is that they are too general to work all the time. If your identity is someone who is good and contributes to the community, your overall direction will be easy to see and follow; however, more specific issues with day-to-day challenges may not be so clear. Whether you feel you have the identity of someone who conforms or someone who is more individualistic, it is likely you will not find approval from people who are at the other end of the spectrum. In other words, whatever we are doing to satisfy our needs, some people will agree with it, and some people won't. It will not work in all cases, and depending on the environment, you will need to make some adjustment. This is an adjustment people will make when they have to. It's not a matter of ability. A good example of people landing in a system they do not otherwise support occurred in the sixties and seventies when many rebellious, individualistic people were drafted into the Army and put into basic training where they were required to conform and work in a system of cooperation and interdependence.

When our environment is strong and directive, we will adjust ourselves to attempt to satisfy our needs in that environment. This is why children respond well to boundaries, and why hostages will start to side with their captors. We will always behave in ways that we believe will satisfy our needs. Therefore it is not so much a matter of our capability to change and satisfy our needs in positive ways. We are flexible, and we can change. It is more a matter of identifying more specific ways of satisfying our needs that we are in control of, that we support emotionally, and give us consistent positive results.

The fact is, we do this naturally anyway. In many cases people do it to extremes and try to satisfy their needs with excessive or compulsive behavior. People who hoard animals may be trying to satisfy their needs for love and connection and possibly significance. Animals are very quick to make us feel important and significant, and they open up in a loving way much more easily than many people do. This can lead us to feel validated: at least some living thing appreciates us for who we are, makes us feel important, and loves us unconditionally.

How about workaholics who spend eighty hours a week on their career? They may be trying to satisfy their needs for significance through their work identity and possibly connection with coworkers and clients. Perhaps they believe that if they are successful, they will get loving connection from their parents, who will be proud of them, or from a love interest, who will be magically drawn to them because of their uniqueness and heroic commitment to their great calling.

Obsessive behavior such as animal hoarding also strains other areas. A great deal of time needs to be spent taking care of the animals. Other people and relationships may suffer because they are not getting the attention that they should. Kids in these environments may feel competition for the love of the parents in relation to the animals. With the focus on the animals' love, the hoarder may stop participating in other important activities, including personal and household hygiene.

The workaholic will likely experience conflicts in time management. Just because of the demands in their work schedule, we can predict that they will have to cut corners in the amount of time they spend with their family or partner, or on their health, hobbies, relaxation, and other ways in which they should also be satisfying their needs and taking care of themselves.

Such extreme vehicles for satisfying our needs will work to some extent *because* they are so extreme. The trouble is, they will work in only a limited way, and are not sustainable long-term. Compulsive behavior tends to be so consuming that many of the person's other roles and relationships will be damaged by neglect.

This shows how important it is for us to satisfy our needs in several different ways. We need to find a balanced approach that is more expansive and leads us to not just satisfy a few of our needs in one category, but rather to satisfy all of our needs, at high levels, in all the areas of our lives that are important to us: career, health, relationships, and others.

By focusing on and satisfying your needs in several areas in a positive, healthy way, you will be more able to deal with unexpected events in some of your other areas. It can be likened to investment strategies. There are two very popular ones, which happen to be opposed to one another.

- Don't put all your eggs in one basket.
- Put all your eggs in one basket, and never take your eye off the basket.

Obviously, workaholics and animal hoarders adhere to the second strategy. We can clearly see this is not the most beneficial way to look at satisfying our needs. Although not as extreme, most people do tend to spend their time in the areas that they perceive satisfy their needs. These areas may be positive or negative. They may enhance the person's life or not. They will tend to be the thing or things the person enjoys, or at least does not want to give up. Bad habits could fall in this category.

A more balanced approach for personal happiness is to find enjoyable ways to satisfy your needs at high levels in all the categories of your life that are important to you. If health and relationships are important to you, then doing even light activities with friends such as bicycling or bowling will be in line with your outcome. By working on several areas at once, you'll reduce a feeling of an unhealthy dependence on any one area.

A main reason we are not good at satisfying our needs is simply that most of us don't have a clear understanding of what exactly our needs are or understand the choices we have in satisfying them. By clearly understanding these nine needs and recognizing that it is important that we regularly experience satisfying them in positive ways, we can raise our level of fulfillment and ability to support and influence others, and do it more quickly, than by any other means.

How would your life be if you had total certainty that you and your life were important and really mattered and you regularly experienced deep love and connection with nature, your Creator, and the people who matter most to you? As well, others expressed approval and admiration at the ways in which you lived your life, and you knew that you were growing and contributing beyond anything that you ever dreamed of?

Well, I doubt you would be suicidal. Surely, when your needs are met, you will have more energy and feel much more alive and loving, and in turn, will want to help others experience great feelings too. It's like the stories you hear about someone doing something kind for a stranger. Both people get some needs met. Let's say a random man on the street gives a random woman a rose and a genuine compliment for no particular reason. She may feel special or significant, or perhaps the kindness will help her feel loved or validated or appreciated for just being herself. His self esteem and sense of connection may rise because he could have an impact on her in this way. For the next few days or weeks, they may both experience increased positive energy from this one simple positive action that met so many needs.

I started this chapter by saying that people are not good at satisfying their needs. This does not have to be the case if we are aware of the needs and the ways in which we can satisfy them, while we assist others in satisfying theirs.

Chapter 29

Awareness of Your Highest-valued Needs

When you are aware of the nine needs, you can make dramatic shifts in your own life as well as the lives of others. You should also notice that everyone values each need at a different intensity—everyone will have the same list, but in many different orders. Lastly, note that the combination of needs nearest the top of each list will dramatically shape the strategies each person uses to satisfy their needs.

For example, if someone has love and contribution at the top of their list, they would likely involve themselves in activities that support satisfying those needs, such as volunteering to work directly with people who need help. We can predict they would prefer jobs and activities that provide a deeper relationship with others rather than a less social environment fraught with turmoil or unhealthy competition. (This person might, however, be interested in improving such an environment.) Another person who values certainty and significance the most might want to have some unique skill that makes them indispensable.

Remember though—it is important to satisfy all the needs, and significant challenges may arise when only one or two of the needs are consciously valued. It isn't the best situation when satisfying the top two becomes so important to the person that they sacrifice the rest. It is not all that uncommon for someone to place a high value on one, two, or three of the needs and at the same time believe there is a great scarcity relating to those needs. In other words, for example, they feel that they are never loved enough, they are never significant enough, or they never have enough certainty in some area of their life. When this happens, it is unlikely that the person will relax and look at things or try things differently to satisfy their needs. It is much more likely that they will intensify their behavior, expecting a positive result. When that doesn't work, they are likely to become even more intense and desperate. By understanding the needs, of course, we can easily turn a situation like this around.

By identifying the highest valued needs in yourself and others, you gain clarity in understanding what Anthony Robbins calls your "driving force." These are the hidden motivations that cause you to decide on the best outcomes and the best ways to reach them based on the order in which you value the needs. This order has a dramatic effect on your life. Now would be a good time for you to write down the order in which you value the needs so that you can better understand where you are in life and why.

When writing out your order, keep in mind that you want to understand how you value the needs in real life, Robbins distinguishes them operationally, rather than rating them as how you would like to see them. Just write down which needs drive you when you're not even thinking about them. If you do this with a partner's assistance, you may be able to benefit from a more objective detached perspective. Remember though, whatever your partner says, even though it is different from what you might say, it needs to be taken as useful insight and not any form of criticism. Start by looking at some of the more important things in your life for clues. Here is an example.

Why do you work? Why did you choose your line of work? If you work to pay your bills so that you do not end up on the street, you may be motivated by the need for certainty. If you work because you don't want that girl you're trying to impress to see you living on the street, you may be motivated more by the need for significance, with love being in the second place. In any case, if you haven't yet done so, stop now and identify the order in which you value your needs operationally. Be honest in your assessment, and if there is a difference in how you are operating compared to how you would like to operate in the context of your overall life, this is the best first step for making that shift. Most of the time, simple awareness of how you are operating and the knowledge you can satisfy your needs even better with a shift is all it takes to change. Start with an honest understanding of where you have been living.

Certainty   _____

Variety   _____

Significance   _____

Validation   _____

Strategy   _____

Goals   _____

Love and connection   _____

Contribution   _____

Growth   _____

Once you have completed this exercise, look at your top needs. The ones in the top five positions will shed light on how you make decisions and why you are where you are on the road of life. Most important are your top two or three needs, as most people are willing to sacrifice some needs to satisfy others.

Looking at your top needs, you may notice how they have affected all areas of your life: why you live where you do, why you have your career, friends, hobbies, pets. Remember that whatever order you have them in, it's okay.

We all have the need for certainty and significance and validation. Many people are uncomfortable acknowledging those needs. Let it go, it's not important. We are not so much as trying to change the order as understand it so it can be used advantageously. What matters is how you are satisfying your top needs. We can satisfy our need for significance in negative or positive ways. We can criticize and belittle others or physically attack them. Alternatively, we can help people on a large scale or be the most significant role model in someone's life. By satisfying our needs in highly positive ways, we satisfy more of our needs, help others to satisfy their needs, and improve our overall environment.

Understanding your needs gives you power, because you can consciously set up ways to satisfy your needs that provide a longer-lasting emotional return for you and others, and you can evaluate your needs better in certain contexts. For example, if you had met your need for significance through your career and now you are satisfying it at high levels through your children, you may be able to change your focus at work to one of creative variety or contribution or something more sustainable and enjoyable. In other words, you can find better matches for your roles, contexts, and needs. It may be a better choice to fulfill your needs for love and connection with family and friends rather than having coworkers be your primary source.

Make sure your needs are listed in the order of how you are committed to operate, and keep it in a place where you can see it throughout the day. By simply having an awareness of which needs are highest, you will be able to use these tools immediately to consciously make better choices than ever before.

Finally, one of the best ways to assist yourself to unify both your conscious and unconscious behavior is to harmonize your values and needs. To start with, you can realize the importance of the needs themselves and commit to making them a conscious priority. Then look at other things or emotional states you value. Once you do this, consider ways that you could experience these states and values directly each day at high levels and in different contexts. For example, if you wanted to experience love as a highest value, there are several things you can do immediately. Just deciding to experience love in relation to the different areas of your life and realizing that it is a priority for you may be a great shift. You could decide to feel love for your career, including the opportunities you have with other people in it. You could experience love with your health by feeling strong and powerful while you exercise or eat healthy or do other positive things to boost your immune system such as simply smiling or meditating on love. You could experience love with others any time you want by realizing you are a fully capable sender of emotional energy. That, of course, means you can experience and share your highest-value emotional state any time you would like, regardless of the states or even the location of others. I know you can think of other things. Whatever you do and in whatever order you value your emotional states, that is what is right for you, and it's perfect.

We just need to make sure our vehicles are as worthy as our values.

Chapter 30

Needs Conflicts As Strategy Conflicts

Once you identify the needs and notice how you and others are operating, you can see areas where some of the needs tend to either complement or conflict with each other.

The need for significance may not complement the need for love. The need for certainty may not complement the need for variety or, more likely, the strategy used to get significance or certainty. Often people who are trying to satisfy their need for significance do so in a way that may alienate others. They may be seen as acting self-important or they may belittle others, thinking they will seem superior or more important than those whose faults they can so easily identify. Even someone giving love while looking for significance may be perceived by others as being someone who is only looking to establish self-importance.

Another challenging area is seeing conflict where it does not exist. Here is a simple illustration. Let's take our two siblings who now are both under ten but only about two years apart. It is not uncommon for some behavioral rivalry to occur to get the parents' attention and be significant. The two competitors believe, incorrectly, that there is one and only one position of favor in the parents' eyes. Often when seeking significance (or any needs), people operate as though the need is a rare commodity: if one person is significant, then other people are not. This is neither true nor healthy. It is better to understand that everyone can be significant in the way that suits them best. A group of people performing well and achieving significance is preferable to one person trying to hold the people around them down to hide their own shortcomings and be viewed as significant.

Competitions based on a shortage of significance can cause damage in family situations, friendships and the work environment, where the ideas of teamwork and cooperation are more important. It is the responsibility of the leader in any of those situations to define exactly how each team member is to participate to be viewed as significant, and clearly communicate that there is no conflict in the roles. In matters of business where competition may lead to job advancement, one could set a specific and appropriate time period. Even then the competition should be for each team member's personal best performance, not to outdo anyone else. After all, a good team player would support the idea that the best qualified should advance and serve the whole team.

Competition for significance as a strategy is well described by a metaphor using a giant clock like Big Ben. This beautiful and efficient system has dozens of gears of different sizes and shapes organized so that when one gear moves and advances, so do the rest. The system works extremely well because each gear leaves a space for the gear next to it to operate. All gears are essential, and if any were missing or in another's place, the system could not operate. By allowing each gear to perform its essential task, the whole system functions in harmony. In a human system, when one person tries to satisfy their own needs without considering their function, role, or outcome by doing the job of another gear to gain certainty or significance, they may be unbalancing the system. It is best to make sure we are satisfying our needs in a way that supports everyone and the larger outcome.

Other internal needs conflicts can arise when someone believes falsely that they can be only one way or another. For example, a person could think they need to always be busy doing something and experiencing lots of variety, and that if they are not doing something, they are boring or will be bored to death. They have trouble realizing that at different times we can appreciate all of our needs without conflict.

There are many such conflicts. If I'm loving and nice, people will take advantage of me, threatening my certainty. If I make a lot of money and become significant, people will resent me and withhold their love. I must choose between a stable relationship or a passionate relationship.

For children, internal conflicts of this nature can produce atypical behavior such as schizophrenic or multiple personality symptoms. When a child believes that they must behave in drastically different ways for each parent and they cannot resolve the two positions internally, the resulting behavior will be an expression of that inability.

Let's take a three-year-old child whose mom's top needs are love and connection, and the mom gives approval and love to the child only when the child also shows she values love the most. In this case she would not treat the child well when the child attempts to satisfy other needs such as feeling important or learning new things. Now suppose Dad is not the emotional type; his number one need is significance. Therefore he encourages the child to stand tall and do important things, and he withholds his praise and attention if she does not appear to be interested in achieving or showing off.

Now let's understand how this is not even the worst of the situation. Small children do not sharply distinguish Mom and Dad. To them, "Parent" is a unified role without boundaries. You probably still remember your grandparents as more of a single grandparent unit than as separate individuals. The very young child is simply not equipped to recognize the value conflict as originating from two different external sources. The child is more likely to try to adjust internally to the incompatible messages. When the parents fight over values and make conflicting demands on the child, the child may become a casualty of the war. As parents we must align for the benefit of our children and agree to support each other's highest values so that the child hears a unified message. This will let him or her know that there are multiple positive values, all of which will get love, attention, and approval from either parent.

With adults, it's easy to see that sometimes we link our identity with our attempts to satisfy our needs. Someone who's trying to satisfy their need for significance might be labeled with the identity of an egomaniac, or someone trying to satisfy their need for variety might be thought of as a careless or unreliable person because they would jump out of a plane. These behaviors are not identities, they are strategies or vehicles that we use to satisfy our needs, and the problem is only the perception or labels generated by others and not the actual needs.

While we may believe the labels are inaccurate, we will nevertheless operate in the way that we believe is best for us in targeting our most valued needs. This could include avoiding behavior that others label negatively. Until we operate from the understanding that it is good to satisfy all of our needs at high levels, and that this can be done without any conflict, loss, or any other problem, we may accidentally link the need with our identity or what it is we are doing and avoid things that would help us and others. What a shame it would have been if Mother Teresa had quit her work fearing the other sisters would shun her for becoming famous.

We can easily change our behavior toward better need satisfaction once we understand what is going on. We can satisfy our needs in positive ways that do not compete with our needs or the needs of others. All we need to do is notice the difference between the needs and how we are satisfying them, remember that this behavior is in no way our or anyone else's identity; it is only behavior intended to satisfy needs. That behavior can easily change to something more productive.

Ask yourself a few questions:

- What behaviors do you participate in to satisfy your top needs?

- Is there a positive or negative identity related to how you satisfy your needs?

- Could you change that identity by clarifying the needs you are satisfying?

- Are those behaviors in conflict with other needs?

- Do those behaviors feel good? How about long term?

- Do those behaviors support other people?

- Do those behaviors really complement and support your other needs?

- Do those behaviors support your roles in life? How about your values and life outcomes?

Were you able to identify some behaviors? We all have self-images of how we would like to be seen by ourselves and others: capable, serious, trustworthy, fun-loving, and countless others. How do you need to be? It's okay, we all have a way that we feel we need to be. It could be who we need to be for ourselves, for our role in our lives, or with other people. We believe being that way will satisfy our needs. What is yours?

Understanding *the way you need to be* will help you understand what your current strategy is for satisfying your needs.

If your strategy is giving you some sort of negative label, it is best to challenge it, meaning if your family has labeled you an excessive workaholic, you would do well to consider they may really be seeking clarity as to which needs you are satisfying. Best to clarify with them that you are a committed breadwinner for the benefit of the family, and your commitment is a reflection of your love for them. Failing to make this clarification could leave a serious misunderstanding of your highest intentions for those you care about most.

If you are stressed and worried a lot, then at least part of being that way is a reflection of an inner belief you have that being stressed and worried is appropriate or helpful for you to satisfy your needs. Perhaps your need is for certainty or validation, so you feel it is beneficial to be on the lookout for things that would threaten those needs, and you engage in worry and stress without even thinking about it. Perhaps your needs are for loving connection, and by being stressed and worried you can commiserate with others and appreciate their caring.

On a higher level, perhaps your entire strategy is not working, your relationships with others are not something you believe you can maintain, and you do not feel fulfilled or have a happy life. So you're stressed or worried trying to figure out what is going on in an attempt to make your life the way you feel it should be. Solving that challenge, of course, is the purpose of this book.

I have two closing observations for this section.

With need conflicts, we should understand that they can occur internally, meaning we can have inner conflicts where our needs seem to be opposing or contradictory. We can also have need conflicts externally, between two or more people, where the needs either do not complement each other or there is a feeling of scarcity, a feeling that there is not enough success to go around.

Fortunately, we can all satisfy all of our needs at high levels in positive ways, once we understand the targets and strategies that we use to satisfy our needs.

Chapter 31

Are Our Needs Good or Bad?

This is a frequently asked question to which I would say: The needs in themselves are neither good nor bad; they are the motivation for our behavior. They are the forces or emotional payoff we receive for our behavior, and by understanding their influence, we can move to the next step, which is to decide how we are going to satisfy them. Everyone must regularly satisfy all of their needs, or there will be some negative emotional fallout. Therefore we should accept and encourage ourselves and everyone else to satisfy them regularly.

Many people will feel a little uneasy about whether it is okay to experience fulfillment of certain needs. For example, the idea of significance may be uncomfortable because it is linked with being an egomaniac or being self-centered, and a person might feel that they or others might reject someone who values that need. Possibly love as a high value does not sit well. Perhaps loving is associated with vulnerability and the possibility of heartache, or a sense that being open and loving others will make people think you are shallow or stupid, which of course could lead to some sort of rejection or exclusion.

Besides, we may satisfy some of our needs by *rejecting* things like significance or love or growth. Perhaps if we reject people who value significance, then we get to see ourselves as the type of person who is more down to earth. (Oddly enough as Robbins notices, this is just another way of showing our own uniqueness, importance, or significance.) We may openly reject the idea of love or the importance of intimate relationships to establish ourselves as knowing better or being enough all by ourselves. Rather than admit that we have shortcomings and have failed in relationships, we can satisfy our other needs by denouncing love as a fiction or a trap for fools. Regardless, the emotion of love is alive in our hearts, and we do experience it with animals, memories, ourselves, places, and many other things. We may reject the idea of growth and take the position that we are doing so well that there is no need to grow any further. Admitting the possibility of room for growth may work against some people's needs to be seen as being enough or being worthy.

The big thing to remain aware of is that it is not the *need* that is good or bad, positive or negative, it is the *procedure by which someone satisfies their needs* that is okay to question. Does the person have a good strategy or not? Are they taking positive actions that make their life better while they satisfy their needs?

When you made your lists of needs and prioritized them, did you notice any negative sounding boards, labels, or feelings of uneasiness about wanting to satisfy any of them? If you did, then likely you stated a need in extreme manner (too specific) or you were too general about what it means to satisfy that need. In either case, is important that you reconsider and find ways that you do approve of to satisfy that need. If you can't think of any, then find someone you respect or admire and ask them how they would look at that situation. They may give you some perspectives or labels that you can agree with, things you hadn't even considered. We all have or can find excellent strategies for satisfying some of our needs. The great thing is, we can borrow from each other those strategies that work.

In the needs game, strategy is everything.

Chapter 32

The Magic Key, A Superior Strategy

Is there a way to align your resources and satisfy your needs in a way that will bring you personal fulfillment?

Absolutely!

Understanding the needs is the first step. Because one of our needs is to have a superior strategy, this is naturally a perfect direction. By understanding the nine needs, we are aware of very clear targets, giving us direct control not only in satisfying our needs, but perhaps what is more important, choosing superior ways of satisfying them.

This is key, because we must first understand and accept that is it okay to satisfy our needs. We should and must satisfy them, and so should everyone else.

Ensuring we satisfy our needs at high levels is the number one feature of a superior strategy. The important distinction is in the vehicle, or *how* we satisfy our needs.

The second step is determining whether our behavior is ecological (sustainable). We can use the following very simple three-question NLP ecology test.

1. Is it good for me?
2. Is it good for others?

3. Does it serve the greater good?

If you are able to answer yes to all three, you are definitely operating at a higher standard than most. Along with answering those three questions, you should also notice if you are satisfying your needs, especially the top few, at high levels. When your behavior and actions support others and yourself while satisfying your own needs, you will understand and reap the benefits of a superior strategy.

The third step is making your outcomes and goals very clear. A strategy without a clear purpose is nonsensical. Just "being" a certain way is not enough, although it could be a part of your outcome. Life is an ongoing process, and for us to do more than just exist, we need to have an end to which we can apply our strategy. Life is movement; it is full of actions that take place sequentially in time and space. Often we operate as though we need to be something or to reach a static goal. We then may be surprised or even disappointed to find our expectations do not match the external reality.

This brings up another fun idea to consider: Life continues beyond the attainment of goals. Typically we are not taught to think beyond goals, and sometimes that leaves us unprepared.

We must have goals to base our actions on. In a general way we pursue them as though they were things or static events. For example, we want to have this or that thing or we want to learn this skill or have that body weight. What we always need to remember is that when we reach these goals, we must face the fact that they are ongoing processes. Once we reach the goals, we must possess and maintain those things that we wanted; we must maintain our strength and weight.

Goals serve us best when we remember that they are like milestones or markers. We should notice and celebrate reaching our goals while keeping our eye on the horizon and being excited about the next goal. Remember that the goal is not a permanent stop on the road of life, because our journey must continue.

When we have a meaningful goal that we are pursuing, we can judge if our strategy is appropriate for our outcome. In this way our internal compass is made active, awakening and elevating the part of our nature required for the new outcome. For this reason, depending on the outcome, it may be preferable or more accurate to associate someone's identity with the way they are currently behaving to reach an outcome rather than to judge them on some outdated past behavior. If someone is committed to their kids' success, we could support this by acknowledging this commitment on the identity level.

Step four is noticing context. When we are considering any strategy to achieve a goal, it is extremely helpful to notice how important context has become. After all, we are talking about behavior, and behavior that is helpful and appropriate in one context may be quite inappropriate and unhelpful in another. Behavior without this ability to adjust is often labeled as infantile. In reality, we have all suffered bad or even disastrous results when we reproduced a behavior that worked at one point in our lives in a new, and wrong, context. Here are some examples of unsuccessful cross-contextual need satisfaction.

Let's say someone is a powerful CEO of a Fortune 500 company. This position will be a vehicle for satisfying many of the person's top needs at high levels: significance, connection, validation. However, when she gets together with the greater family for the holidays, the same behavior that makes her successful in business may backfire, because the family may not react well to being treated no differently from a business underling.

Take a person who considers himself highly sensitive and who is aware that he over-worries about ludicrous things. He has also learned that certain others accept his behavior and reassure him that he is loved anyway, resulting in feelings of importance and validation. This is clearly an impoverished need-satisfaction strategy. If he carries this behavior into the workplace, there's a good chance he will cross some boundaries of appropriateness. That could lead to a missed promotion or even job loss.

Intimate relationships are fertile ground for such inappropriateness. When a man regresses in an intimate relationship and expects his wife to take care of him in the same way his mother did, there are problems, and we have all probably seen them.

By checking that our strategy is context-appropriate, we can be much more sure that we can satisfy our needs at high levels, and we will more clearly understand the challenges we see in the relationships of others. Plenty of professional therapy is centered on nothing more than identifying and changing behavior that is part of an out-of-context strategy.

Needs Purgatory

There are a few things to look out for that can be traced back to needs challenges.

Violent behavior is usually due to a belief that a person's needs are unable to be met in a valued relationship or circumstance. This may be due to very real circumstances, such as another person not being available or willing to participate in the way the person desires. If the person feels their needs are being blocked or there is an injustice associated to the needs deficiency, violence may seem reasonable to the person. This is not the same as someone who may be aggressive, yet respectful.

1. Over-focusing intensely on one particular need can create an imbalance that is unlikely to be supported by other people and may cause the person distress. Someone consumed with one need like certainty, validation, love, significance, or variety where the need

seemingly cannot be satiated may have trouble relating to people with a more balanced need requirement.

2. Strategies of failure. If someone's underlying belief is that none of their needs are met because of their tough lot in life, the emotional costs for maintaining such a dismal outlook will be very high.

3. No goals. The habit or practice of not valuing goals. To somehow believe it is better not to set a goal, versus the practice of consistently planning future events in a way that excites one.

4. Disassociation. The habit or practice of representing things (or others) in one's life as being separate, distant, or unimportant (beneath them). It is not caring about things that should be cared about.

5. Superiority or contempt. The habit or practice of predominantly acting as though you are superior to others. Often displaying contempt for them and this attitude may be accompanied by an unwillingness to be forgiving.

Chapter 33

It's About Unlocking the Needs

For simplicity's sake, let us call a superior strategy one that regularly satisfies the needs of others and yourself at high levels, remembering, of course, that need satisfaction is an ongoing process and not a one-time goal.

You also want to release any concerns that there's anything wrong with satisfying any of the human needs. If you have any inner conflict centering on a feeling that it is not in your best interest to experience things such as variety or significance or love, it is best to address those conflicts directly. Chances are that certain needs are being considered in either an unnecessarily general or a too specific manner, not taking into account all the ways highly appropriate ways to satisfy those needs. We will be talking more about those; they are what make up a superior strategy.

The next thing to notice is that it is okay for everyone else to satisfy all of their needs at high levels. In an environment where everyone is satisfying their needs at high levels, people tend to focus more on others and the positive things can be done, rather than being negatively preoccupied with trying to satisfy their own needs. One of the fastest and most effective ways to satisfy our needs is to help other people satisfy their needs. When we use our time and abilities to visit with someone who needs company, or mentor a young person, we may simultaneously satisfy all of our own needs. Additionally, we are operating from a place of abundance where our own perception of ourselves is that we are more than enough and we can share freely of ourselves. This is an important perspective because it helps us operate in a positive, healthy way, and it empowers our relationships with others in many ways, perhaps most notably in the way it allows us to reduce our demands and expectations of others.

It is also important to realize that there are always enough positive emotions to go around. They are in great abundance. At times most of us haven't given this enough thought and operate as though we must compete for significance. Is this true, though? Significance is a feeling or an emotion; it is not a commodity or something tangible or scarce. Same with love. We hear people say all the time that they have given all the love they can and they have nothing more to give. Love is an emotion too; it is a feeling we create. If we are going to run out of any particular emotion, I would think that depression would be a better emotion to run out of, especially given its negative effect on our lives.

Of the needs, significance, validation, and love may be the three that can cause the most disharmony in our interpersonal relationships. This typically comes from the idea that there's some competition for the ability to experience that emotion or that we can be taken advantage of if we display some emotional kindness towards someone and it is not reciprocated. The fact is that we can love others freely for our entire lives without negative consequences. Besides, the quality of our lives is much more likely to be positive if we give ourselves permission to be loving. This will also solidify our identity as a loving person.

With an understanding of goals and context, plus the knowledge that we are working with emotional states, let's explore some empowering strategies for more specifically satisfying each of our needs at high levels.

Chapter 34

Strategies for Unlocking Each Need

Goals

The major reason for setting a goal is for what it makes of you to accomplish it. What it makes of you will always be the far greater value than what you get (Jim Rohn).

Of the needs, goals are a natural place to begin because they are such an important part of our thought processes and influence so many other things. You may wonder why I placed something like goals at the level of a need or emotional target. I did so because something I have found personally to be true is also consistent with the viewpoint offered by people when questioned about what it is they really want in life. Surprisingly, it isn't more money or more significance. Besides love, the most universal experience people are seeking is what they define as "meaning and purpose in life." I suggest that because we have free will, we may select worthwhile goals, simultaneously giving us purpose and defining meaning for why we are here. Simply put, goals can equal meaning and purpose. Exercising our free will by moving towards well-chosen goals is like having a master key to meaning and purpose in your life.

We would do well to realize that whether we are aware of it or not, we do have goals. If we have not set conscious goals, our behavior will still move naturally in the direction of the goal of satisfying our needs, meaning we always have goals: the unconscious targets of certainty, significance, love, and all the rest. Unless and until we move consciously to satisfy these goals, our unconscious conditioning will do the job, with mixed results.

By understanding the nature of goals and consciously deciding what goals are right for us based on the ultimate feelings, experiences, and outcomes we want for our lives, we can also consciously arrive at more thoughtful and all-around better ways of reaching our milestone outcomes. Indeed, life is a journey and can only be experienced as a process, yet nothing defines who we are and what we are doing better than the positive outcomes we are committed to achieving.

As to goal setting alone, there are many excellent books on that topic readily available to you, so I will spend the rest of our time focusing on considerations specifically related to strategies and needs.

Start with the Big Picture

It is helpful to take a broad look at the rest of your life and notice the upcoming natural stages and transitions that you can and perhaps should set goals for. It is more helpful to set goals that you can accomplish rather than holding the carrot out just beyond your reach as a fixed, yet never attained, target. When you set reasonable, attainable goals that are defined so clearly that you know with certainty when you have reached them, then, by acknowledging yourself appropriately when you do, you will soon experience momentum and "juice" towards those things you wish to experience in life.

The broad view will take into account markers of physical development: learning to walk, growing teeth, riding a bicycle, reaching puberty. Whether or not we state our goals, we do have expectations for how life should be or what we should have accomplished by a certain age. Biological clocks play a role, such as the urge to have children before reaching the age when problems in childbirth begin to occur more frequently. Though there is a typical progression for goals by age (marriage, finishing our schooling, having kids, retirement), we do love the stories about someone going back to college after retirement or jumping out of a plane on her 90th birthday. I definitely encourage questioning any idea that suggests something cannot be done because the life stage is "wrong."

The "right age" for doing anything is not the focus. Becoming aware of your own expectations for your life and planning your goals around them will greatly assist you in evaluating if you're doing the right things to reach those outcomes in the time frame you would like. This type of planning can greatly reduce or eliminate the midlife crisis syndrome where someone suddenly realizes that they will be changing life stages and they have not yet experienced or accomplished some important parts of their life plan.

By looking at the big picture of your expectations and goals, you can also more easily notice if there are possible conflicts, and if you are inflexible as to some of your outcomes, you can make sure you clarify that with anyone you are considering becoming a life partner with. It can be very problematic in a relationship when one partner is committed to some particular outcome more than the relationship. It is best to make things of this nature a team effort, which of course requires disclosure and planning.

Sort Your Goals into Categories

After you have mapped out your big picture goals, you can move down into categories:

- Career
- Family
- Health

- Spirituality
- Intimate relationship
- Anything else that is important to you

Then go through the categories and superimpose them one at a time onto the big picture of your life in progressively longer time frames: a week, a month, 1, 2, 5, 10, 20, 30 years. Your whole life will come into much better focus, and you will be able to, at any given time, know where you are and where you're going.

Choosing Your Goal Achievement Strategy

Once you've identified what your important outcomes are and the time frames in which you would like to reach them, you have arrived at the most fun part: here you get to decide the best strategies for reaching your outcomes. It is important to remember that there are no limits to the means by which you can reach your outcomes, only the limits of your imagination and commitment. It is useful to acknowledge and use your internal flexibility when deciding what vehicles you will use to reach your outcomes. Of course a superior strategy for reaching your outcomes will include the idea that you are positively satisfying all nine of your needs and that you are doing so in an ecological manner: it feels good, is good for yourself and others, serves the greater good, and is sustainable.

How are you doing about now? I wouldn't be surprised to hear you say something like, "Hey, before I read this I wasn't even sure I would reach my goals, and now you are adding specific conditions on top of everything else?" Well, okay, it's true, there are just a couple more things to consider upfront, yet the result is that you are more likely to enjoy the process of getting to your goals, which in turn will increase the likelihood that you will stay on track until you reach them.

Here's how you might do that.

Perhaps two of your outcomes are to get into a long-term relationship and find a career that will provide income to support your other goals. Doing this process makes it easier, because you will have a valid system for determining which choices will support and fulfill you long-term.

Let's say you are a woman, and you want to determine if your boyfriend is good husband material: family, kids, and all the rest. If you are in this relationship because he is kind of a bad boy and you like all the variety and excitement, you might want to accept that a relationship with such a self-focused man will not support your bigger picture. Devalidating him, trying to change him, may not be a realistic plan. Turn this around into a search for somebody who shares your life plan in a stable way while also sharing your passion for variety and excitement, someone who is a great fit in all the areas important to you in your future.

Same in choosing a career. Let's say you have just been offered a job, and you have a sneaking feeling that you are probably going to hate it, but it pays great money. This can be tempting, because you might be telling yourself that if you do well enough in this distasteful job, you will just bite the bullet in the expectation that you will still be able to satisfy all of your other needs in other areas. Your important title and hefty salary will make you feel important and significant, many people will approve of you, and you can then satisfy your needs through those people.

However (bet you knew there would be a however), because of the importance of a positive self-view and the amount of time we spend in our careers, it is much better from the beginning to evaluate your career or position relative to your nine needs, especially your top three or four, as well as to do the assessment about whether it feels good, is good for you and others, and serves the greater good. Having a career that satisfies these criteria (your criteria) will have you feeling much better about yourself than a position that either satisfies only your need for significance or certainty or one that gives you plenty of love and connection yet does not pay you enough to properly care for yourself. Just as an employer screens prospective employees according to certain criteria, now you can empower yourself to screen your goals for how they satisfy this important set of criteria. Making these distinctions will change your life dramatically.

Time to Think about Time

Now, to wrap up this talk about goals and a good strategy, I would like to share a very helpful way to understand how the unconsciousness of the goal process may have both hindered and helped you in the past. As we learned earlier in this book, the asking and answering of questions relating to a goal directs us to a certain answer that we take action on. The important point here is that we must notice how all of our goals are placed somewhere in a perceived time frame, which could be short, medium, or long term. This occurs whether we are conscious of the goals and time frame or not. For example when you ask yourself a question relating to food, part of your internal question and answer session will bounce the idea off an internal sounding board. That sounding board will have considerations about time frame. If you are considering ordering a hot fudge sundae even though you are also trying to lose weight, your ultimate decision will be based on whether you are focusing on the short-term pleasure of having the sundae or whether you are sounding the idea off your long-term outcome of losing weight, being fit, and so forth.

Short-term goals   Medium term goals   Long-term Goals

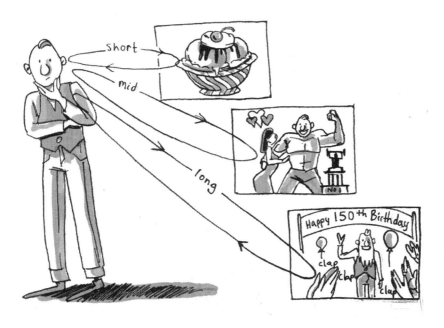

This diagram illustrates the loop of our current thinking on how we prioritize and internally map short, medium, and long-term time relative to our outcomes and our behavior. Our decisions have built-in time frames that affect our long-term outcomes. If you have been consistently disciplined or successful for a good length of time in some area of your life, we can be sure that your decisions in this area have a long-term time frame. If you are physically fit and maintain a healthy weight, we can say that your choices around food and exercise are not based totally on immediate payoffs, but rather on outcomes you wish to ensure in the future. Many people have similar time frames around career skills, intimate relationships, and other areas. Too much focus on one time frame, even long-term planning, can have a negative effect. Perhaps we neglect our overall well-being when we suffocate short-term pleasures for ourselves and those close to us.

At the other extreme, if most of our moment-to-moment questions are answered based on outcomes of immediate pleasure or avoidance of pain, with no consideration of a more positive long-term outcome, there will be an imbalance. It is easy to see how drug abuse, smoking, overeating, or other compulsive-distractive behavior reflects an unconscious high priority on a short-term goal. Even people who are aware of these patterns and have begun to break unhealthy habits of improper eating and exercising may relapse or cycle between healthy and unhealthy behavior depending on what time frame they are focusing on.

Is there some part of your life that is causing you problems, where you really want to make some changes? The easiest remedy may be to make sure you are making decisions in that area based on your most desired long-term outcome. Anyone who overeats regularly is clearly basing their moment-to-moment decisions on what to eat based on a short-term benefit of feeling good. At the same time they are *valuing* that short-term outcome more highly than the avoidance of the long-term consequences of overeating.

A good strategy understands this and makes appropriate use of time with goals. It thoughtfully prioritizes long-term goals so that short-term action supports us in reaching these goals. At the same time, a good strategy allows us to experience pleasure consistently in the short term in a way that reinforces medium and long-term success.

Certainty

While goals are usually something tangible, and we have some evidence to tell us we've attained them, certainty is often only a feeling we have about something. When we feel certain about something, although it may be based on some fact, it is only an emotional association that we may take some action on. We feel certain we will be with our partner forever, so we share some secret that, five years later in divorce court, makes us wish we had kept our mouth shut. But we had a feeling of certainty at the time, and a desire to operate from the standpoint that our relationship would endure, and we planned around this and invested ourselves in it.

How Can We Be Certain?

We may not think of certainty as an emotion. We are more likely to think of it as the occurrence of wished-for events, such as "When I have enough money I will be able to relax knowing I'm okay," or "When I find true love I'm certain I will be fulfilled forever." But uncertainty can still exist, even when all our bills are paid and our savings account is healthy. Even when we have found the love of our life, we may still live in fear that it will not last. These statements illustrate the "sounding boards" we have set up for deciding when we should experience the emotion of certainty.

These sounding boards also tie in with goal setting. When we say we are going after money or true love, we unconsciously assume that attaining these things will fill our emotional target of certainty. Let's say you want "true love." You sign up for a dating service, meet a likely prospect, and date for a year. At some point you may want to be certain you have found true love. The only way you can do this is to check with your internal sounding boards about what to expect when a goal has been achieved. These sounding boards are different for everyone. Certainty could be a feeling, a look, a touch, or something our partner says. It could even be someone whose opinion we respect telling us that this relationship is definitely true love. Maybe it's several of these things, or even all of them.

By understanding more specifically what our sounding boards are, we can make more specific goals in line with our lives, which will add a huge amount of certainty that we will understand and experience our most sought-after emotions. Let's consider you want financial security. You could ask yourself, "How will I know when I have financial security?" What is my certainty sounding board, idea or rule? When you do this, a couple of interesting things may happen.

One is that you may have a challenge with time. In other words, let's say you're 20 years old and for you to know you have financial security, you need to have $50 million in the bank. Right now, however, you have nothing in the bank and $1,200 in credit card debt. Even if your financial target were only $25,000 in the bank, you may find you would experience years of financial uncertainty while you take action towards becoming financially established. Some people believe that it is good motivation to raise the bar of what it will take to satisfy their need for certainty and set million-dollar goals. Unfortunately that strategy does not allow you to move forward in time with certainty as *a successful person.*

Let's look at people who are earning a great deal of money. Do they do it with confidence in their ability to be financially success-ful, or do they do it freaked out in a desperate attempt to satisfy their need for certainty? These are two very different attitudes. To illustrate, let's take a look at those people who have risen quickly into the millionaire category and then lost it all. There are several accounts of people who start over with nothing and quickly match and surpass their previous financial benchmark in a fraction of the time it took them the first time. Some of them say that the first go-round gave them the confidence and certainty they needed to suc-ceed in the next one. Of course, others in that situation may have been motivated mainly by a wish to avoid the uncertainty of pov-erty, while yet others were motivated by a combination of those feelings.

We can easily predict which of those positions would give someone a more rewarding emotional experience: the one with confidence and certainty, of course.

When you try to satisfy a need by setting up rules to establish or maintain motivation, but which are tied to a goal you cannot realis-tically accomplish, this may miss the mark for being the best strategy. Unless you are fortunate enough to have good success during the short time that the motivation works, it is easy to find the path you're on not rewarding or enjoyable and experience increasingly more negative emotions relating to your outcome, be it in love or money or whatever.

On the other hand, if you maintain your $50 million goal, yet allow yourself as you go down the path toward it occasionally reseting your rules for feeling certainty, you could build momentum for the ultimate goal with interim goals that allow you to experience the certainty you crave and support your identity as a successful person. For example, when you're 20, your actual best actions towards making $50 million may be in educating and developing yourself or entering a field that has the potential to bring you your returns in the time frame you believe to be realistic. Once you have mapped out your year-to-year path to your goal, you could change your rule system to ensure that you consistently feel certainty about your outcomes. After all, you are on track and you are doing the things you've decided will bring you your outcome. The feeling of certainty along the way should keep you committed.

The other interesting thing is that many goals that are related to certainty tend to be very large, usually much larger than what is really needed. We don't say, "I need $50 million to satiate my need for certainty," we just have a feeling that we would feel a lot better if we had $50 million. (We might be trying to satisfy other needs beside certainty, but let's focus on certainty right now.) So if we decide to set a goal of $50 million based on *certainty*, it may be helpful to understand more specifically why that goal is important for us. If it is because we do not wish to be poor, than the number may be unnecessarily high. Perhaps there is a more specific goal that we may already have a sounding board for that we could more easily achieve certainty about. Maybe having your house paid off and twelve months' living expenses in the bank would make you feel just as good or even better, especially if you really felt you could do it.

By evaluating and knowing for yourself what it will take for you to experience certainty, your goals will become much clearer, and by having graduated, achievable steps, you will not only be more likely to reach your milestone, but you'll experience the full emotional juice that inspires the goal along the way.

Certainty Is Essential for Moving Toward Goals

We must have certainty to even function as thinking human beings. People who suffer from hallucinations and delusions cannot plan at all because they suffer from uncontrolled, threatening perceptions. Many suffer extreme anxiety as they attempt to consider the possible responses to an incalculably high number of possible threats. For us to operate without a way to filter out meaningless information and choices is to accept irrationality.

Not only do we need certainty that we are evaluating valid realistic information, but we also need certainty that the number of choices we are considering can be reduced down to a small enough number that we can make a final selection for action. That is to say, we need to have the emotion of certainty in our ability to even make choices. Many people would call this weighing their options. We weigh them for soundness and probability, and we must eliminate some of them with certainty. We then need to experience the feeling of certainty towards one or more of the remaining options. If not, we may be paralyzed by indecision.

Certainty Is a High-Priority Need

Of the nine needs, certainty is in the top three for most people. For many, it is the top need or very close to love, validation, or significance. People who value certainty at a high level tend to prefer environments with very little change, or predictable change. Because of that they will stay in relationships longer and will have fewer job changes. They will invest in infrastructure and support systems for long-term thinking and success. Humanity has advanced in countless areas due to the actions of those looking to satisfy their needs for certainty. When considering a long-term partnership, whether in business or some kind of personal relationship, it may serve you well to notice your prospective partner's relative valuations of certainty versus variety.

Certainty Occurs on a Spectrum

If we are to look at certainty as a useful value, it is helpful to notice that at its best and most useful, it is confidence: confidence in our abilities and judgment. On the other end of the spectrum, it is the need for control based on fear.

Confidence---------------------/---------------------Fear-Based Control

The fear is that we are "not enough" or not able to handle unpredictable variables in our environment. People do not always operate from the most useful position on this spectrum and may be stuck on one end or the other, to their detriment. Confidence needs to be based on an appropriate assessment of ability. On the other hand, people suffer unnecessarily from fear of things that are entirely out of their control. In its proper measure, certainty is definitely a need that we will try to satisfy in our lives. It is also an extremely valuable emotional resource for thinking, future planning, and peace of mind. The choice to be certain (positive or negative) with our emotions that we can or cannot reach a goal is more of a decision then actual reality. As Henry Ford said, "If you think you can do a thing or think you can't do a thing, you're right!"

Certainty Can Be Used to Control Others

A great strategy recognizes the emotional value of certainty for ourselves and others. It also recognizes the harm that can be done when we seek to control the behavior of others by withholding certainty from them. In intimate relationships, for example, it is quite common for one partner to attempt to change the other partner's behavior by threatening to take some action that would cause a great deal of uncertainty for the other partner: ending the relationship, leaving, taking away the children, or anything the partner counts on. In some cases one partner will even threaten suicide.

Children are especially vulnerable to being controlled by need for certainty. We must recognize their uniquely high level of the need for certainty due to their dependence on others for their physical and emotional well-being. To an adult, some uncertainty may not seem like a big deal because they have a basic measure of understanding and control. A child, however, is not only reliant on others but also less familiar with the context in which statements are made. If a parent says something like, "If he comes home late from work again, it's all over," the child may have trouble grasping the true limits of the statement, hearing only an all-encompassing, "It's all over." That may be very emotionally disturbing for the child. Fulfilling the child's need for certainty with constant and appropriate reassurance will help give the child the stability needed to function in a healthy way.

Children are reliant on their parents and those around them to help satisfy their emotional needs. They also need some certainty that what they are doing will assure some success in satisfying their needs. Parents need to recognize that it is important for both parents to be aligned with each other and agree which behaviors will receive praise or positive attention. If a child is praised by one parent for certain behavior and given disapproval or punishment by the other parent for the same behavior, the child may develop some inner conflict that they have trouble sorting out. Sometimes parents do this to use the child as a pawn in their own battles. Young children in Western cultures are typically not able to distinguish any hierarchy in parental roles. Such mixed messages create a great deal of uncertainty regarding how they can satisfy their needs. In extreme cases, unhealthy behavior can be a result.

Control by way of the need for certainty occurs in the workplace too. Either the employee or the employer may try to influence the other based on removing certainty. Either way, threatening to quit the job or eliminate the employee will cause resentment. If the other party values certainty at a high level, they may not be able to emotionally tolerate continued uncertainty and find it necessary to change or leave the environment. By being clear to the party who requires certainty as to the expectations necessary for certainty in the relationship, that party will receive the control they seek and are motivated by. The requirements absolutely must be things that the other party is fully capable of achieving, and they must be allowed to succeed in restoring their sense of certainty.

Of course these types of withholding behaviors cause more damage and destabilize the relationship, primarily since we strengthen a relationship when we help the other person to satisfy their needs, and we hurt the relationship when we block them from satisfying their needs. If you seek to help others satisfy their need for certainty by helping them, you will help your environment, and ultimately it will serve you and the greater good.

Variety

Variety, the spice of life. The difference that makes the difference.

Just like certainty, variety has more to do with our emotional state rather than actual conditions. We set up in our mind circumstances definitions or sounding boards for what has to happen so that we can experience the emotions we associate with variety. Of course these conditions or ideas change over time. When we are in an exciting new career or relationship, we tend to believe that it could never get old or boring. Then, imperceptibly, it becomes the same old same old.

The exciting thing has not changed, only the our *feeling* about it. When this happens, almost undoubtedly what you are doing is generalizing about the situation and looking at the big picture while ignoring all the detail. You ignore what is different. You think your spouse always does or says the same things, and you are bored to death with him or her.

Robbins Says "Be Curious!"

Fortunately, we are more in control in this kind of situation then we may realize. The first thing to understand is that we can experience variety any time we want. One of the fastest and easiest ways to experience it is to become curious. If we believe we know everything about something, it is probably because we are only looking at the surface of the subject.

Curiosity is an also a great strategy for satisfying our needs and helping others do the same. Remember the feeling you experienced when you felt someone was genuinely curious and interested in you? This creates a profound connection and communicates to others that we appreciate and value them. The fact is that every person on the planet has some unique perspectives or experience that has given them valuable knowledge. By being curious, you will give others the gift of your interest, and you may receive many gifts too, including valuable insight.

Don't your kids or spouse or parents all deserve a fresh look? Instead of having your mind made up about who they are, realize that they have changed since you first knew them, and your initial opinion may not have been 100% complete. Ask questions! Who do they admire most? What is their greatest or most desired accomplishment? Try to really know them and care for who they really are. Perhaps you could reverse it. Do you feel that your parents, spouse, or kids really understand who *you* are? If you say yes, then you are lucky. The doors of variety are there for us to open. All we need to do is focus our gaze on the things and people that really matter in life.

Empower Yourself With Variety!

Besides getting curious, you can directly empower yourself to experience variety. When you enter an intimate relationship, you try to understand the other person so that you can establish a blueprint for what it will take to maintain stability and certainty in the relationship: do's and don'ts, partner's likes and dislikes. Often these initial judgments become fixed perspectives that may not be accurate, yet still restrict the choices we feel we have. It's always cute to see long-term partners arguing about what the other likes or doesn't like. Or haven't you been in a situation where you feel you cannot be yourself because someone has stereotyped you: others expect you to behave according to a certain pattern, such as a being a bad cook, when in truth you have learned to cook gourmet dinners!

Dr. John Gottman, the marital therapist, researcher, author, and professor at the University of Washington, promotes the idea of "love maps." A love map is based on the idea that our perceptions about our partner and our relationship can be likened to a map. We know who they are on an intimate level. We know their capabilities and things that are important to them. We also know about their day-to-day environment, who they are involved with, and what they are doing. Working with his wife Julie (also a marital therapist), Gottman proposes that one of the key components of a healthy relationship is regular updating of love maps. When partners lose touch with each other's self-identity, what's going on the other's world, what's important to them, then they are moving apart. Conversely, and perhaps an even more important revelation, when couples expand their preconceived maps and are willing to accept that their partner is changing over time or that they may have had it inaccurately or incompletely the first time, they give themselves the gift to grow and build the relationship.

Sometimes when people change, it's hard to see, meaning we need to try even harder to stay in touch with those changes. Milestone events occur in the lives of a couple, such as having kids and grandkids, deaths, career changes, but we still may not recognize the changes and growth in ourselves or our partner. With children it's a little easier because the changes in physical development are more obvious. Noticing even subtle changes supports others in a helpful, loving way. This way of satisfying our needs for variety is not in conflict with any of our other needs.

Maybe We Can Live Without Variety -- But Is That Really Living?

Many of us at one time or another operate under the belief that if we were to bring certainty to our most important areas of life, we would be fulfilled. There is never absolute certainty in life. There is quite a difference in the quality of someone's life who values certainty above the other needs and someone who learns to value satisfying their need for variety. Calling it the spice of life is a good analogy because, just like spicy food, we do not need to pursue this need as directly as most of the others. However, without it life is bland, and enjoyed in proper measure in the right contexts, variety can make all the difference in the world.

Everyone Can Experience Variety

Key to experiencing variety is recognizing our ability to do so. Most people are able to experience variety, but they tell themselves they are not: I don't have time to do this; I can't make this other person feel happy; I used to ride a bicycle but now I can't do that anymore. We say these things even though they're not true, and after a while we start to believe them. Don't let that happen, or at least catch yourself and reconsider what you're really able to do.

Variety Has Variety

Another great thing to remember about variety is that, as we move through the different stages in life, the ways in which we satisfy our need for variety must change in order for us to satisfy all of our needs in a sustainable way and with a sustainable strategy. There are some things we can do our entire lives, and then there are things that need to be updated so that we are making the most of the point and time in life we are at now. As an example, middle-aged people who are attempting to relive their long-lost youth typically do not feel any better having made the attempt, nor do they receive the good judgment award from their friends and family. Applying variety to itself and making sure we are doing things that are life-stage and context appropriate are part of an excellent strategy.

Significance, Self-worth

Significance is the need we all have to feel important, special, unique, or that we matter. This is another high-drive need that for most of us is in the top few needs that we seek to satisfy by our behavior. In spite of the fact it is a natural target for us and that we share this need with many other members of the animal kingdom, this need, more than any other, carries with it some negative associations. People are often given negative labels when they try to satisfy their need for significance: egomaniac, showoff, know-it-all. These labels create a contradiction for the person trying to satisfy their need to feel important. After all, being ostracized with a negative label is the exact opposite result that the behavior was attempting to generate.

Why Do We Have the Need for Significance?

We could explore this question by looking at the benefits satisfying this need has had, both for natural environments with animals and with adaptive human environments. One symbol that has meaning in both human and animal environments is the one chosen to represent the most successful traditionally animated film of all time, *The Lion King*. It is the majestic lion high on a ridge set against a magnificent landscape and powerful sky. While the meaning is open to interpretation, I believe some universal things can be read into it. Does it not evoke our primal emotions, not only to survive, but to succeed and excel as a natural intention, to stand tall without ego, celebrating our victories in this extraordinary undefined process we call life? Is it even perhaps healthy to recognize and celebrate our abilities so that we may put them to use them for our own and the greater good? It is perhaps odd that in our society it is generally more permissible to notice and focus on the negative aspects of life and failures of ability, versus celebrating what is right and our ability to make things the way we want them.

Is there a way for us to see the positive benefits we can bring to the world while satisfying our need to feel significant? Can we bring out the best in ourselves in a healthy way, enriching the planet, each other, and future generations, simply by changing our perspective on our belief of the intentions behind our behavior?

Do we not need to acknowledge that most of the advances in civilization over the ages were, in great part, done to serve the need for significance? Kingdoms were made in the names of the leaders and the special people associated with them. New lands were explored, charted, and claimed in the name of some leader or his people. Legacies were left as markers by those who wished only to not be forgotten. Countless advances in math, sciences, astronomy, art, human understanding are made when this drive to be significant, to excel and achieve, is combined with the desire to grow and contribute with a loving attitude. When this happens, we will be living in a way that not only supports more people but is also much more sustainable for future generations. The need has been around a long time and is not going away anytime soon. Let's find positive, sustainable ways it can be put to use.

How Do We View the Need for Significance with Children?

At an early age, children seem to form beliefs about significance, usually associated with the belief that significance implies a sort of comparison, that if one thing is significant, then perhaps another thing is not. That being equally significant is not as good as being more significant than something or someone. There are often ideas of scarcity about significance. Beliefs that the "commodity" of significance can be exhausted can lead to intense competition within the family for attention based on fear that the "losers" will not get their needs met, creating jealousy and bad feelings. This is scary for kids, who require plenty of assurance.

It is natural and not wrong for children to have a desire for attention and approval. They are merely seeking to satisfy their needs, and quickly find that behavior which is loud, animated, or demonstrates some uniqueness will get attention. The rules will vary in different families. If such behavior is disapproved of, a child may learn quickly that being too significant can lead to pain or an undesired result, and therefore they may avoid being too significant. If they then try something else but are not rewarded with attention and positive emotions, they may go back to the behavior that at least got them attention, because they may link more pain to being ignored (not significant) than to being punished, for which they do get attention.

Children who are praised and given attention for developing a particular attention-getting behavior may likely identify with that behavior and seek to get better at it as part of an overall strategy for satisfying needs. In other words, if the child makes the family laugh by doing funny things, the child will feel reinforced and internally approve of the behavior as a surefire way to satisfy his or her needs. If we take any actor or comedian and ask them about their childhood, we will most likely learn that there was a point in their youth when they decided being an entertainer would satisfy their needs, and the decision was based on reactions in that environment.

Role Models Tell Us How to Be Significant

There's a similar story for anyone who has developed a particular interest or skill. If you ask them about it, you can discover how it was reinforced, or find out that they had adopted the behavior of a role model who they would like to have had the approval of. One of the major appeals of any role model is that people believe the role model is satisfying many of their own needs at high levels. We notice popular actors or musicians and see that they feel significant because they are loved by millions, seem to have attained certainty because of money and social status, are validated by all of their fans, and get plenty of variety. Therefore we would like to either be like them or in some way be associated with them, or do the same things that they do so that we can be just as happy as they are.

Other role models may be our parents or someone else who seems to have things figured out. Of course, some role models are of a counterculture type, those who satisfy their needs by being significantly different and blazing their own path, charismatic rebels who burn themselves out by their unsustainable choices, or rebels who influence and connect with enough other rebels to reinforce each other and satisfy all their needs (conforming rebels).

Most of us also have the tendency when looking at role models to arrive at the belief that if we are significant enough, this significance will be a great vehicle with which to satisfy all of our needs. We somehow assume that wealth and fame must naturally lead to happiness and success. Of course not all rich people or entertainment stars are happy in their personal lives, nor is it a given that they will satisfy all their needs at high levels. In fact, it is more likely that high significance-producing positions bring unique challenges to successful need satisfaction. Self-destructive behavior, suicide, and rampant drug abuse are the negative vehicles many "successful" role models use to satisfy their needs. Even so, we still keep believing that if we had that type of significance, that sort of advantage, we could avoid the pitfalls of success. Some of us continue to believe that that significance is an end in itself, a worthy goal that will bring us fulfillment.

Parents Tell Us How to Be Significant

Many parents attempt to get their children to adopt their own values, and validate strategies in the children which they use to satisfy their own needs. Many parents see this as a gift of identity or as a sharing of the internal recipe for how to make life work. If done with love and positive reinforcement, the values may transfer to the next generation easily. A good example would be the mother who has had a fairly picture-perfect life: homecoming queen who married well and wants her daughter to be Miss America or at least Miss Minnesota. If the daughter is consistently reinforced positively for entering princess contests, learning to dance and dress like a little princess, the princess values will transfer to the daughter, who will experience a positive identity and feel successful satisfying her needs in this way.

If, on the other hand, negative behavior control is used, the child will be in a position where she cannot win and likely will attempt to reject the values at some point or another. If the mother is impatient and critical of the child to gain short-term compliance for long-term benefit, the child will likely rebel, feeling that there is no positive way to satisfy her needs, and that by rebelling she will at least satisfy some of her needs and send a request to the mother to change her approach. Of course the mother is asking the daughter to change her behavior by withholding the daughter's needs.

This kind of negative control is, of course, also is a major problem in intimate relationships. Whenever two people withhold needs from each other to control the other, there will be problems. We will talk more about that and how to solve those problems before we conclude here.

Positive Significance

In a greater sense, the need for significance is our desire to have some sense of purpose, perhaps to be needed or understood by others or to know that our life matters or that we are making a difference. Because of this, if we choose to satisfy our need for significance in positive ways that people easily recognize and understand, and we do things that matter while making a difference, we will be in tune with our underlying need structure. After all, it is easier and more rewarding to live a life of meaning and purpose than to live your life only looking for meaning and purpose.

It is said that one of the greatest gifts you can give is the gift of your attention or presence. I think this statement goes a long way to explain how we can easily satisfy our needs for significance in the best way possible. When we step back and take a good look at our lives, we can more easily notice that who we are, where we are, and what we do are relative to many different people and roles we have in our lives. Because we are in a unique position relative to some people of being the most important or one of the most important persons in their life, we may not be noticing or paying attention to at the level we could. We may have too easily given up on relationships in which we do not believe we can satisfy our needs, yet in actuality they could be the most important relationships we will have in our lives.

Our most significant interpersonal relationships are, of course, child, sibling, spouse, and parent. These relationships hold the highest possible place of significance for us and the others involved. When we acknowledge the importance of these relationships and seek only to give to those closest to us the gift of helping them satisfy their needs and the gift of our presence, we will complete the relationship, and we will have met all of our needs, including our need for significance, at a fulfilling level. These gifts do not, of course, include the gift of our expertise in noticing what is wrong with them. They are the gifts of appreciating who they are, validating them, and being present with them without judgment but with acknowledgment of the strategies from which they operate.

Balancing All Relationships Is Important

After our nuclear family relationships, we of course move out to other roles and relationships: extended family, career, community, friends, hobbies. People who are satisfying their needs at high levels are usually doing so in only one or two categories. Sometimes they are satisfying their needs in only one category, and because of that they are spending too much time there and the other categories are suffering. For example, if somebody is not satisfying their needs with their spouse and family, yet they are competent and appreciated in their career, they may prefer to work late versus going home. This type of situation creates an imbalance, and there are likely to be some negative consequences. If we choose to consciously find ways to satisfy all our needs in these various roles and categories by growing, contributing, and helping others to satisfy their needs, we will move to a greater sense of balance.

You can easily make a list of your most important categories. Most of us will have the same list How can you best satisfy your needs in these categories?

- Health

- Family

- Intimate relationship

- Career, mission, or purpose

- Friends

- Hobbies or interests

- Other things unique to you

Now list ways that you can satisfy your needs in those categories. Let's explore the idea of balance between need satisfaction categories by picking one of the needs, significance, and let's start with the category of health. You might be asking, "How can I satisfy that category through health?" Well, without health you will be dead, so there's not much to argue about there; you need health, and so do the important people around you. Perhaps by making better dietary choices or finding activities that are not only great fun but include some physical exercise, you may become a significant influence on others in your immediate environment, causing them to notice and begin to take better care of themselves. Your challenge is not to make others feel insignificant because they do not adopt your values, but rather to merely do what you know to be right and hopefully provide a positive role model that others will learn from. You may not realize the impact you have. If you are 45 and you start exercising, your kids may not jump on the bandwagon with you, and yet, when they turn 45, they may decide that they should begin to exercise and plan for their future too, just as they saw you do. Never underestimate the significant benefits that you can set in motion by your positive actions.

In your career category, perhaps you can define what excellence would be in your role and then commit to making that your standard. By holding yourself to a higher standard, you will feel better about yourself, having established a new reference point or sounding board from which you can judge your own identity and abilities. Additionally, if you have made the adjustments to your behavior in a way that supports others, the entire organization should reap the benefits of your direct action. Also, you may inspire others to understand that they can satisfy their needs by giving of themselves in a spirit of positive cooperation.

Our closest relationships with family and our intimate partner are probably the most troubling, yet most important, areas for us to apply this principle and work on satisfying the needs for significance. It is very rare for anyone to feel or experience consistently the emotion of significance at a level they most desire. It is more common to experience the emotion of feeling insignificant or as though we are not enough and therefore will not be loved. With this understanding, we can start to see that in those relationships where we don't feel loved, important, or significant, that feeling most likely reflects an equal belief from the other party in the relationship that they are not enough and that they are not loved by or important to you. That begs the question, do you express to others how important they are to you? Do your parents know of the effects they've had on your life and your positive feelings, or have you shared only your disappointment in their shortcomings? Do your children understand the positive changes that occurred in your life due to their being born? Do they understand the pride you feel or the hope you have for what they may accomplish in their lives? Have you spent more time sharing your personal sacrifices or fears relating to their incompetence or possible bad luck? The wounds of abandonment run very deep for many, whether it is parents who've abandoned children or vice versa, or whether the abandonment was physical or purely emotional. Never underestimate how important you are to others or give energy to the false belief that you are not enough to help others satisfy their needs, just the way you are.

Was there a conflict or misunderstanding that occurred a long time ago with someone that you are still putting energy into by suggesting that the other party is wrong or otherwise not worthy of significance? Will you recognize now that making them wrong will not improve anything, and that only by finding out the good intent that they do have and restoring their significance in the family system can you expect them to be interested in the idea of participating again. Meeting your own need for significance by restoring healthy identities and relationships within your group is another excellent way to satisfy your needs. Tying your own outcome to someone else's success is very different from attempting to satisfy your own needs at the expense of someone else.

Finally, and perhaps most importantly, we must notice and remember that significance is an emotional target. It is something we choose to feel based on our own rules for what needs to happen that then allows us to feel significant. That is why some people will feel significant when a particular thing happens, and yet when the same thing happens to someone else, they may feel embarrassed or experience a different emotion.

Robbins asks people to consider their rules for when it's okay to feel our desired emotions. This is a great exercise because it makes you aware of things like other people in the broader environment as they relate to how you feel.

What are your rules for experiencing the emotion of significance? Take a few moments with a pen and paper and ask yourself what has to happen in different contexts (categories) for you to feel significant.

- In your intimate relationship
- With your children
- In your career
- Other areas of your life

Add as many areas of your life as seem to be important, and then come up with five or ten rules in each category for what has to happen in order for you to allow yourself to experience the emotion of significance.

Are some of your rules based on what *others* need to do? In other words, does your partner need to drop on the floor when you walk in the room and begin crying "I'm not worthy" at your feet before you will feel significant? Is this realistic? Does your partner know that you have this rule? Are your rules something that are kind to you and others, and is there any chance that your rules will be met consistently and easily?

The great thing about your rules is that they are yours, and you can change them. Can you see that you will serve yourself and others much better if you are satisfying your own needs at high levels? By experiencing positive emotions regularly, you will have more energy and be more available to not only enjoy your life, but to also give of yourself and support others in a meaningful way.

So create new rules! Such as, I feel absolutely certain that I will experience the emotion of significance whenever I'm using my best judgment as a parent, spouse, or any other worthy role that I commit to. Or, I will experience significance knowing that the love I give to my family is unique and comes from a very special place in my heart. Have fun with this. Create rules that enrich your life and allow you to celebrate regularly. Remember that the celebration is the allowance you give yourself to experience positive emotions. We all have a full emotional range, and most of us believe it is okay to set up rules that prevent us from good feelings and encourage us to amplify and experience over-intensified negative emotions. This type of thinking isn't supported by medical evidence. Stress, depression, anxiety, fear, anger, sadness, and guilt weaken our immune system and are important factors in many health issues such as premature aging, and even death. On the other hand, there's much documentation supporting the idea that healthy positive beliefs and emotions promote our actual physical well-being.

Our next section is on contribution, bringing up that making a significant contribution can be one of the greatest ways to satisfy our needs.

Contribution

For clarity we are using a single word to describe each of the needs, yet we all have different impressions of what these words represent, depending on how we use them and our past experience. For some, contribution might be teamwork, or selflessness, or mentoring, or volunteering, or even something completely different. There are many different categories included in different people's emotional targets of contribution. Of course all of these would be acceptable definitions of contribution, and I want to make sure ours has is the sense of putting energy into something greater than and outside of ourselves, making a priority of helping others satisfy their needs, either directly or in support of an organization with a greater sense of positive purpose.

Contribution's Place in the Needs Hierarchy

The need for contribution, along with the need for goals and growth, differs from the others. Most people may not invest those two with quite the same intensity or drive. Especially when we are not satisfying our other needs at high levels, then we may believe that our position will be made even worse if we contribute. After all, if we contribute, we will have less than we do now, which may not even be enough to get by on. It is true, of course, that that we must first have enough of whatever resource we need to maintain ourselves before we can contribute to others, in the same way flight attendants caution us to, in case of emergency, affix our own oxygen mask before helping anyone else. If we are incapacitated, we cannot care for others, and we will add to the burden of those who remain capable by requiring their assistance.

This principle applies strictly to only physical survival, however. Even so, for many of us there is a tendency to react to negative feelings or emotional pain in the same way we react to actual physical danger or distress. We may feel it appropriate to take care of ourselves first, just as in the airplane example. While this may seem like the right thing to do, we must not forget that we are dealing on an emotional level only, and that contributing with our positive emotions, and perhaps our time, may be precisely what we need to move out of our own anxiety or depression and satisfy our needs in positive, productive ways.

Contribution Is An Emotional Target

Remember, contribution, like all the needs, is an emotional target. These are emotional states and feelings that bring us a level of fulfillment when we experience them regularly. Because they are *emotional* targets, they have little to do with our actual environment and more to do with our perceptions about that environment. This is why some people regularly experience fulfillment, and some people do not. It is just as easy to experience anger, jealousy, self-doubt as it is love, appreciation, self-confidence, growth, or contribution. There's a tendency to overvalue negative feelings because of the belief that by experiencing them we will prepare ourselves or benefit in some other way, such as coming to terms with the negativity. We therefore sometimes hesitate to shut them down or replace them with more desirable positive emotions. Perhaps by understanding the value positive emotions have for us, we will empower ourselves to fuel up and keep them alive. After all, most people prefer to experience positive emotions, even though many find it easier to indulge in fear or worry on a daily basis.

There is also a bit of a cultural appreciation toward negativity. We are typically better accepted and understood if we take things seriously when we are going through a tough time. We are more likely to be treated well by others when we are down and feeling bad than when we are feeling fantastic and emotionally strong and positive. When we are in public and we see a group of people being loud and happy, we may suspect they are unintelligent or intoxicated, and certainly lacking in proper decorum. What do these things tell us about how we should behave or what states would benefit us?

Why We Need to Experience Contribution

To better understand the breadth of our need to experience the feeling of contribution, it is important to realize that not only do we live our lives with others, but we have always been dependent upon one another to perform various roles essential for our quality of life and our existence. When we are young we are completely dependent on others for our survival. Man-made systems—families, extended families, industries—are built on the idea of working together with loyalty and contribution to provide nourishment and employment, community, nationality, and humanity. It is widely accepted that someone who communicates and interacts positively in all of those systems is a healthy individual, and someone with conflict and negative emotion towards others and avoids them is maladjusted. It is obviously contradictory to reject the very systems we count on for survival.

It would be great if everyone understood why contribution is so important that we are justified in classifying it as a need—something we must experience. When we give of ourselves emotionally and contribute, we are making several statements. We are acknowledging not only our own emotional abundance, but also experiencing the feeling that we have a surplus that we can give to others and still be fantastic ourselves. We may believe, rightfully, that by helping others we are reinforcing and replenishing our own emotional base. By such actions we are experiencing our capability and abundance. We are also expressing approval and support for others and the greater good, we are discrediting doubt and fear, and we are taking action confident that we can produce a positive outcome.

Contribution also puts us in an important position relative to ourselves and the world. As we move out of the complete dependency of early childhood, our world changes as we find our strength in and make the natural transition to the identity of a competent contributor. Intentional contribution could begin as early as age three or four if there is emotional willingness. Contribution is not based on environment or physical capability. Even people who severely handicapped or not fully functioning some way need to be allowed to satisfy their need to contribute to others. Caregivers must understand the importance of contribution as a two-way street, even if the contribution is "only" love. In truth, love is possibly the highest and best contribution anyone can make to another.

The very best way to contribute to others is to help them satisfy all of their needs at high levels. We must also remember that contribution is one of the needs that is self-reinforcing or can be used as a vehicle to satisfy most or all of our other needs at high levels. That's why so many of us do things like freely contributing anonymously for long hours with no pay. Remember, the act of contribution creates a very rich needs fulfilling environment.

How Am I Experiencing Contribution?

Think about that for a moment. I am sure there are areas in which you made an unselfish contribution, and you enjoyed doing it. On a scale of 1 to 10, how well did you satisfy your needs for

- Loving connection
- Growth
- Certainty
- Variety
- Significance
- Contribution
- Goals
- Validation
- Strategy

Was meeting a goal involved in your contribution? Did you feel validated, as though your strategy was correct and reinforced a positive identity for yourself? If you enjoyed the experience and perhaps continue to do it, it is very likely you met at least four of these needs at a level of six or above, probably even higher.

A caveat: It is important to remember that in the spirit I am talking about, contribution means contributing beyond yourself. If you are only contributing to satisfy your own needs, you are not really contributing, you're trading, or expecting your needs be met by others. That is not really contributing; it could even be taking. Contributing means giving with little or no thought of return for yourself, but rather focusing on others or the greater good.

Is There a Downside to Contribution?

For some people, contributing is a little scary because they feel just a tiny bit vulnerable when they contribute. This is due to the perception that our ability to contribute correlates with our identity or worthiness as a person. We fear that if our contribution is seen as being on the "low" side, we might be ridiculed, judged negatively, or even rejected by others. To avoid a potentially painful experience, many people will be reluctant to put themselves in that position. For that and other reasons, many people prefer to contribute outside of their immediate environment, neglecting their relationships, roles, and responsibilities with their closest family members. This is unfortunate, because (in my opinion) we should look first to our own roles in life, our own systems, to expand upon and satisfy our need for contribution. The overall health of any system can be gauged by how well the need for contribution is being met by the members of the system. This is true whether we are talking about a family, a business, an army, or a nation.

What Is the Best Way to Experience Contribution?

While we all have different roles, we also have many similarities and many past reference points to work from to identify how exactly to satisfy our needs for contribution. We all have a role with our parents. Many of us will have roles with brothers and sisters, children, or extended family. We can find role models of those who have contributed in all those categories with excellent results.

It's the same for our career. When we look at role models and people who have achieved the extraordinary, we notice that the ones that are celebrated have contributed over their lifetime in a way that is very meaningful. How would you need to behave in your career to match the identity of someone who would win a lifetime achievement awarded for their contribution in your field? Maybe you don't need to take it that far. Maybe it is just a useful exercise that can give you some ideas on things you can do to experience contribution through your work, and very likely simultaneously help yourself and others satisfy their emotional needs.

Sometimes one of the best ways to grow and contribute is to increase your own standards and improve yourself so that you are being the best you can be. If you're the best parent you can be, it will benefit your children. You may even unknowingly inspire others by being a role model of excellence. Contributing also gives some sense of fulfillment to your parents by helping them realize the almost universal desire for their children's success.

These are only examples of ways to set in motion the positive domino effect of contributing. Start with yourself and raise your standards. Before contributing elsewhere, check your own systems. Are you a good friend, spouse, parent, neighbor, team member? By performing better in these roles, not only will you satisfy your own needs for contribution, but you will begin an upward spiral of achievement that will benefit you and many others.

If you experience inner resistance to contributing to someone because of a long-standing deficit in their contribution to you, this may be an ideal place to start contributing to them. Chances are the other person feels the same way about you. Withholding from others in hopes they will become more generous seldom works, and usually only makes things worse. Better to find your own nature as a contributor and stop fueling an emotional standoff. That is not to say you should allow yourself to be taken advantage of or mistreated in any way. You can contribute intelligently, even if only through reduced negativity when talking about or dealing with that person.

Remember also that there is a flip side to contribution. Everyone needs to contribute, be part of something, and serve a greater good. Because of this, it is extremely important that you allow others the opportunity to contribute to you. Many people, especially "people helpers," tend to experience some discomfort when others offer them any kind of assistance. It is important for active contributors to understand that they are helping others when they allow them to contribute.

Equally important is remembering that we should not expect people who have not asked for our contribution to believe that our contribution creates some sort of relationship in which they must participate. True contribution cannot ever create obligation on anyone's part.

Growth

Our emotional need for growth can be satisfied in many ways. Refer to the Contribution section for some ideas, mainly in the areas of self-improvement where you already play an important role, such as family, friends, hobbies, career, physical and spiritual well-being. This is where you can push yourself to expand your capabilities and understanding. The fact you are reading this is a very good indicator that you already have an appreciation for growth. So what are some good considerations for growth relating to our overall strategies?

Growth in Intimate Relationships

Growth is essential in an intimate relationship. Without growth the relationship is either dead or dying. A relationship where only one person is growing is also either dead or dying. People are most commonly driven apart when one of them continues to grow and the other one does not. Growth can be blocked by a needs conflict, such as a feeling that it is better to have comfort and certainty than growth, perhaps with the belief that growth could compromise certainty. Worse yet are the perceptions that growth yields pain, or that stagnation is comfort. People who feel this way will defend their right to do and be nothing new.

It is important to keep the forward momentum of growth alive in your relationships, especially your intimate relationship. The partners do not need to have the same interests or grow in the same way. However, both parties should be growing somehow and emotionally supporting each other in the process. Over the life of a relationship there are many milestones full of opportunities and challenges. Whether you're honeymooners excited about building a relationship together, new parents, homebuyers, or great-great-grandparents, you can always get energized about improving yourself as a role model for your children and all your descendants, as well as honoring your spouse with gratitude. The opportunity for growth is always available.

Growth In Your Other Social Relationships

It may help to notice that all of life boils down to our relationships with people. While we may have an emotional feeling towards things or accomplishments, this is a different kind of valuing, and things are still related to other people. Let's say you, along with all the material possessions you ever desired, were dropped down on an otherwise unpopulated planet. There you could enjoy your possessions to your heart's desire. It wouldn't take very long before your emotional dependence on people became very clear. So aren't relationships the most important thing in life to improve?

How Can You Measure Growth?

Remember that healthy growth is best measured against yourself: how much you have grown from where you were before. This rules out the idea of unhealthy competition with others or attempting to make others seem less worthy by criticism and such.

Here are some categories of growth worth considering:

1. Improving your inner self by learning new information and skills, developing your current interests, and improving your own physical well-being.
2. Spending your time and resources outside of yourself, including helping other people. To a large degree, your quality of life is measured in the quality of relationships you have. Intentionally growing and cultivating relationships is a great way to satisfy the need itself.
3. Expanding your overall awareness and perspective on the world around you. You may have not even considered this category. This type of growth is, of course, the result of many different types of growth. If we pursue expansive thinking and elevated perspectives as a direct goal, we may find it easy to increase our growth more effectively than we had previously thought possible.

The main thing is to have fun and realize that, to a large degree, we just need to recognize that each day brings us immeasurable possibilities for learning and experience that are always available, should we choose to notice.

Validation

Validation is an extremely powerful need. We need to know that we are doing the right thing in any situation, and that our information is sufficient to lead us to good decisions. It is painful to feel that we are not good enough. This need to know that we are right can be satisfied in more than one way.

Internal or External Validation?

A major reference point for positive need satisfaction is how we view our own ability to satisfy any particular need. It isn't exactly the same for all needs. In the case of certainty, for example, if a person felt in control of how they satisfy that need, they would be able to use a fact (or rule) such as lasting five or ten years on their job as sufficient indication that the job is secure. Other people in the same situation may require an outside action from another person before they feel certain. They may require regular reassurance from their boss at each performance review, or possibly even more often, to feel certainty their job is stable or secure. When we have unrealistic expectations of others for satisfying our needs, it is likely we will frequently experience the pain of not having our needs met. If you need a boss who reassures you before, during, and after every project and takes you to lunch on your birthday, you may run into trouble. Some bosses are willing to do this, and some are not, or they may be willing for a while but eventually feel that your need for reassurance is moving outside of the scope of the relationship.

We all have a different comfort level in deciding if it is okay to feel that our needs are being met. Relevant questions are, do we use our own internal sounding boards? Do we believe it is best to require others to give us their opinions about how we should be feeling? What is our comfort level with external messages that our needs are being met? This comfort level may vary based on the need being considered.

Both validation and love are emotions that may revolve around our relationships with others. So we may feel it very inappropriate to feel those feelings without the expressed agreement of others. On the other hand, some people can feel loved based on how others treat them, even if the loving communication is not direct. In the case of validation, some may feel validated knowing they are living their life the way their grandparents or someone else would appreciate, that is, they have adopted some rules that confirm their right to feel the emotion of validation, and even though it originally came from an outside source, it is now a soundboard within their control.

In any case, when we understand for ourselves the rules we have for when it is okay to experience an emotion, we can have positive control of the process. What about when we do not believe we have control of the process? What we would notice here is whether we have rules that require specific external behavior from others before we allow ourselves to feel the feelings of love, validation, certainty, and so on. So what specifically are these sounding boards? What specifically has to happen? It is common for people to have all sorts of rules that are very unlikely to occur. Going back to our example of job certainty, some like to hear from at least four people per day that they are doing a good job. Even if that happens, they might discount the validation, citing some ulterior motive. After all, you wouldn't want feel all good for no reason at all, right? Besides, reality rarely exactly matches our sounding boards.

Here is my point: With any need, the more control we have in satisfying it and the less dependent we are on others for our own happiness, the better the likelihood that we will feel emotionally satisfied. Of course, relationships with others are essential, and it is also essential to feel capable of maintaining healthy positive relationships with others. What is important, though, is to have our own rules that we understand and have intentionally made for experiencing our most important emotional needs. Make sure your sounding boards match the things that are likely to occur.

Self-Validation

With our need for validation, a good strategy to satisfy it is to do a bit of self-validating. Of course this isn't always productive. People who are having problems will validate themselves by finding fault with their environment. Even if they find fault with themselves, they will feel validated by that as the only explanation that makes sense. The point is that healthy validation does not accept the justification for behavior that is of a lower ideal, no matter what the circumstance. When we do not accept the lesser of two evils but press on, insisting on a positive outcome, we will find it easy to validate our own choice and actions.

Healthy self-validation begins with looking at how well your life is working. If it is working extremely well, then it would be appropriate to validate yourself. After all, it is good to recognize yourself for doing things right. All of us will from time to time have relationships or other things in our life that might not be doing all that fantastically well. Don't beat yourself up or invalidate yourself for those, but rather empower yourself to do the best you can. Work on solutions and give yourself the validation for empowering yourself in this way.

The true test is this: Is your life working or not? If it is, then you deserve to give yourself a pat on the back and encouragement to stay the course. With so many areas of life, such as health, relationships, and career, it is very likely that at any given time one of these areas will be operating below an optimum range. This is okay, and if you recognize this, you deserve your own validation. You noticed the problem because it violated your own personal standards, which are very likely excellent. When you take action or even commit to operating in a way that satisfies your own rules and standards, any inner conflict will disappear and you will feel deserving of your own validation.

That very line of thought would suggest that there are always areas in your life that *are* going well or even wonderfully well.

Make sure you take the time to appreciate yourself for your part in your successes. This can strengthen you and give motivation to also improve the other areas. When you know you can find the emotional rewards in all areas, it is much easier to invest yourself positively.

When dealing with problem areas, rather than withholding good feelings from yourself until that part of your life is in such good shape that you'll never have to think about it again (which cannot be done, of course), simplify the process! While considering your outcome, decide on some small steps you can take immediately that will realign you with your standards and desired outcome. We can, without intending to, take on so much that it is no longer possible to focus, and when we feel overwhelmed, it is all too easy to justify not even starting or giving up.

Helping Others Get Validation

As with all the needs, a good strategy with validation is to help others satisfy their needs at high levels. For many people, external validation is something they have longed for and valued at nearly the same levels as significance or love. Most of us do not receive very much external validation. Remember though, we are all running our strategy; it is our best attempt to operate in a way that will satisfy our needs. When our partner or closest family and friends do not validate us, or worse yet, invalidate us or show contempt, this can drive us to desperation. Decide for yourself where you are invested on the heart level. Which people and relationships are the most important to you? Commit to helping them satisfy their needs, beginning with the need for validation.

What identity do they have that you appreciate?
What values do they have that you appreciate?
What beliefs do they have that you appreciate?
What rules and convictions do you respect and appreciate?
What part of their strategy do you love, or could you love if you wanted to?

Validation is an important need for people. You should never underestimate the impact you may have when you help people truly feel validated.

So if you were to become excited about the human needs and helping others to satisfy their needs, and I hope you are by now, let's say you decided to volunteer on your local crisis telephone line. You would be helping others who are feeling suicidal or otherwise in crisis. You will, of course, need to receive some training. It is very likely that the main skill you will be taught is the art of validation. The entire training will be focused around "active listening" and "validation," that is, really listening to what another person is saying and doing so without any judgment of them. You are to just be present, listen, and repeat back what you think you have heard to get the clearest sense of what they're saying. Once you have really heard them, you agree that their emotional response is understandable, given their story. You validate their feelings as being appropriate. This is a useful and important skill, and most of us do not use it. In ordinary conversations, most people interrupt others and don't listen well. Sometimes we tell the other person they are wrong to have their feelings because they don't understand what's really going on, and we then try to enlighten them into a new and better strategy (like ours). Please note: When someone already believes that their strategy is not working, the last thing you want to do is tell them their perceptions of reality are wrong. It is far better to validate them for what they're doing right and help them build goals for a future based on their positive beliefs, their good feelings towards others, and their ability to select and achieve goals and outcomes.

The Dangers of Devalidation

One of our most common ways of validating ourselves is by correcting others. Unfortunately, this is usually done with the people closest to us who matter the most. After all, we are usually perfectly nice to the letter carrier or our child's teacher. We wouldn't want them to think ill of us, right? When it comes to those closest to us, we tend to be nice to them by pointing out their imperfections (for their own good, of course). Not so nice is withholding their needs, or trying to influence them by making them feel invalidated or insignificant, or making them feel they will lose certainty or love if they do not comply with our wishes (which of course are superior).

A large reason couples separate and divorce is not a lack of love or compatibility. Often it is due to an escalation of a battle in which partners try to get their needs satisfied by withholding the other person's needs. As this process escalates, with both feeling justified that they are giving or willing to give more than the other, the relationship dies, and the partners find other ways to satisfy their needs. This can be through such things as kids, hobbies, work, or a new partner.

In many close and intense relationships there is withholding of approval or validation as a way to communicate the fact that some behavior is making the de-validator unhappy, or at least not creating happiness. When a parent finds that withholding approval from a child gets the child's cooperation, the parent may turn withholding validation into a pattern. There is plenty of negative fallout from this type of situation. The child could satisfy the validation need in other ways and with people who are not as concerned with child's future, possibly people that the parents see as negative influences. The child may get some satisfaction by distressing the parent(s) with this behavior.

Using withholding validation in close relationships can get even more negative when a rule develops around the withholding, a rule that becomes outside of the unvalidated one's control. If a parent withholds approval for academic performance unless the child gets As and Bs, without realizing it the parent may adopt an inner belief that they can only be happy with the child when these conditions are met, and be unable to let down this "guard" even when the child tries harder and begins to earn satisfactory grades. The result of, course, is that everyone is miserable. The child feels that nothing they do is ever good enough to win the parents' approval, and the parents feel as though the situation is never right or stable enough for them to relax and be happy.

The same type of thing happens in intimate relationships when one or both partners display a negative disapproving attitude, a permanent frown that tells the partner they need to change something before the disapproving partner will be happy. Even if the criticized one tries to change, the frowning attitude persists as leverage to maintain the desired behavior. This is not sustainable long term because the disapproved one will not receive validation from the relationship, and will never feel that they are doing enough to make their partner happy. In a relationship that is healthy and growing, it is important for each partner to know that their presence is desired by the other. You need to know that you make a difference, and that just by being yourself you can make your partner happy. If you never get to believe you can make your partner happy, or worse yet, believe that your presence makes your partner miserable, the relationship is going the wrong way.

The antidote for such misery, and a good strategy, is to reverse this process! Make sure the people closest to you are being validated and appreciated for their own special uniqueness and the unique way that they look at and deal with the world around them. They can get your approval and make you happy just by being themselves and not necessarily doing anything extraordinary. The old saying is true. When people can win with you, you will win with people. You will never win with others or influence them long-term by making them wrong all the time.

Include yourself in this process. Many people make themselves perpetually "wrong" in an attempt to create the drive to take some positive action. What they end up with is a life spent in a bad emotional state. It is better for your health and your long-term results to motivate yourself positively by validating yourself and building on your successes. Right now might be a good time to remember that validation is an emotion you can choose to feel. Could you take a moment to reflect on all the positive things you have done for yourself and others throughout your life? Think about how proud the people in your past would be if they knew how well your values have shaped up. See them appreciating all the good things you intend to do with your future. Quietly allow yourself to experience, possibly more strongly than you have ever done, the emotion of being totally and completely validated. When you have that feeling, feel free to double the strength and expand it to include appreciation for not only your life but also your relationship to everything in it, now and in the future.

Love

Start by making the experience of love a goal. By making it a target that is within your capability and that you're committed to experiencing, you will empower yourself to satisfy one of mankind's most profound needs and desired states.

Feeling Love

Attainment of this experience is under your control. Some people do not believe this. If asked what has to happen for them to feel love, the items they list will be extremely rare or hard to reach, perhaps some very specific behavior from others on a regular basis.

It does not serve us in the long run to support the beliefs that make feeling loved difficult. When you make it easy for yourself to experience loving states, you will come to remember yourself as a loving person, and that identity is more likely to influence others in a positive way.

Go beyond making it one specific goal. Make it a goal that you are certain you can achieve easily and regularly. Love is very flexible and multidimensional. We have opportunities to notice and experience different types of love in different situations or environments. By being able to satisfy our needs with several vehicles, we will be more emotionally resourceful and avoid the feelings of emotional depletion.

One way is to start very large and work your way down in the categories of life. In other words, take a moment and remember a time when you had a great love for your life and your existence. Now re-experience it. Seriously, decide now to take the next few minutes to fully associate and relive that experience as though it were happening now.

Then remember another time when you felt love for a deep connection with your Creator or nature or the earth, or each one individually. Then re-experience those loving feelings. When you're at the peak of those experiences, notice the exact feelings, sounds, and images that accompany those feelings. Notice them in a way that will allow you to remember then re-associate at any time you like with those feelings.

Who in your past influenced you at a heart level? Every one of us has experienced a connection emotionally with our own heart level core strategy and someone who touched or inspired us in some way with a loving sense of self. How does it feel now to allow yourself the gift of re-experiencing those feelings? Even if that person or situation is no longer around, the gift of that experience is always there for you.

Now let's look at another level of your existence, let's say your career. At some point, perhaps when you were starting out, you felt a strong emotion towards your career. If it was a loving connection, great! Re-associate to that now. If not, imagine how it would feel if you felt love and fulfillment towards what you do. If any urge to stop pops up, tell it to go away, because you are playing a game right now that requires you to associate loving feelings towards all areas of your life.

Continue going through the roles you have in your life and the relationships you have with people. Even if you have disconnected with a family member or someone else who matters to you, allow yourself to feel love for that person and gratitude to that relationship. If the relationship is with a child, sister or brother, or parent, that means you have an identity or role as a parent, sibling, or son or daughter. Be thankful for this life which has allowed you that role, and allow yourself to experience love and gratitude for that opportunity, even if that relationship is not "perfect."

Work your way down to smaller levels of things you love and that you are grateful for: a favorite movie or book, the feel of sunshine on your face, something in your house that makes you smile, something you always keep close to yourself. Maybe a pet? Of course, for some people their pet would be a high point that they would start with. There is no wrong or right. What you see as global or large, working down to small, is yours alone. Whatever you do is perfect for you.

The main thing about experiencing this type of positive emotion is that you make it not only okay, but that you make it a necessity, one which is possible and within your control to experience regularly. If we merely wish to feel good and hope that circumstances will align so that these feelings will somehow just happen, yet we take no action, we are far less likely to experience them. It is much better to embrace as our own this positive human desire for something that we all need to experience and then empower ourselves to experience these feelings directly.

How about the opposite? Wouldn't it be great if there were a complex set of very specific rules and events that had to occur in a precise order before you could allow yourself to feel negative feelings such as sadness, guilt, fear, or anger? Culturally it seems acceptable to justify having negative feelings without any real reason. Let's turn things around. Unless you want to experience those negative emotions regularly, perhaps you could make a shift and have simple sounding boards for feeling the emotions of fulfillment, happiness, appreciation for self and others, and of course, love.

Giving Love

Another great strategy for satisfying your needs for love, as well as several others, is to open up and recognize that you are a *source* of love. Allow yourself to be a giver. Develop self-awareness of the emotions you are projecting towards others. We all experience and emotionalize our responses to the people and situations in our lives, yet not all people have the same reaction to the same people and events. They make a choice: Do I like this person or this situation? Or do I have bad feelings towards this person or situation?

Now here's where it gets interesting. Let's say that I dislike someone I have just met; perhaps I have an unpleasant feeling of disapproval. I may believe it is best to reinforce who I am as a person by letting my disapproval be known. This could protect me if I'm fearful or do not want to be bothered. In other words, I believe some of my needs will be met by this behavior.

Where this begins to be a problem is when we generalize and believe that we will satisfy our needs by experiencing these types of negative emotions in most situations. By presuming the worst in our environment, such as believing that most people are untrustworthy, we may believe that we will be prepared to handle a negative challenge, or at least we will not be surprised by it. It's as though we have negative feelers out into our environment. If we do find negativity there, we may become even more negative. The problem is that we will tend to continually experience those negative emotions. We could call such an attitude pessimistic: negativity until proven otherwise. The optimist, of course, assumes positivity and abundance until proven otherwise. A very big difference between the two positions is that pessimists usually believe that challenges will be more than they can handle and cause uncontrollable negative results. Optimists minimize the likelihood and severity of challenges, with the empowered self-view or belief that they can easily handle or even prosper from any adversity.

Just like the pessimists who believe that their view of life helps them to satisfy many needs— certainty and stability, significance because they have a great grasp of the seriousness of the problem, validation for the way in which they handle it—so too do the optimists believe that they satisfy their needs through their optimistic view. They feel certain they can handle anything, they feel significant by the superior way they handle crises, and they feel validated as they implement their superior strategy.

So is it better to be optimistic or pessimistic? It seems pretty clear that being in the extreme in either direction is not beneficial in the long run. Being unrealistically confident in truly challenging and dangerous situations will likely leave you unprepared in those few critical moments. Also, being too pessimistic will take its toll on an emotional level. Science has proven that excessive amounts of time spent in states like anger, sadness, fear, and guilt often result in illness. Such costs, whether physical or emotional, are not worth incurring, given that we live in an environment that is relatively safe and predictable. Keep this in mind: Just by assuming that bad things can happen and preparing emotionally by feeling negative, we are not reducing any risk or overcoming anything.

The obvious choice seems to be maintaining a healthy ratio of positive and negative emotional states. What is a healthy balance? There are no exact numbers available for individuals, but John Gottman, the relationship expert, has shown that for a healthy relationship between two people, there needs to be a specific ratio of positive to negative to preserve the relationship, and it is not 1 to 1. It seems that much more positive than negative energy is required for balance: at least five parts positive to one part negative emotion. Negative emotion appears to be highly toxic.

These numbers are quite astounding, and should lead us to ask ourselves pointed questions about our relationships. Do we presume five times out of six that the other person has a positive intent? Do we expect that our interaction with them will be beneficial or detrimental? How about with our coworkers or our customers? It seems we may be more willing to be optimistic and treat our customers very favorably because we know if we do not, we will have lose business. The same principle applies in our relationships with our closest family members, yet for many it is easy to have a negative expectations of them, such as having ulterior motives for behaving kindly toward us. We know that this critical view is bad for the relationship, because it invalidates the other party. Still we keep doing it, because we believe that that is the best thing to do to satisfy our needs. If we were to treat our spouse and children as though they were our most valued customers, we would have better relationships with them. Isn't that what unhappy couples are? Robbins calls them people who have been manipulated by negative expectations to the point of being fed-up, unsatisfied customers. Of course in a relationship it is hard to see the forest for the trees, and therefore it is not unusual to blame the customer instead of looking at your own self to gauge whether you are adding value to your customer/partner.

To be a source of love and positive emotion, you must realistically expect the best in the intent of others and in your own ability to handle situations. Often love is experienced and expressed as appreciation: appreciation for life, appreciation for any number of things that make up our experience and that we are grateful for. We can always remember to appreciate others. We can appreciate who they are now and who they have been. We can appreciate what they bring to the table with resources or good energy or just plain positive intent. There is an old Japanese proverb: "A retainer who does nothing but think positive thoughts and wishes only the best for their employer is still a worthy and trusted retainer." So it is that we too can value and appreciate others who do no more than wish us well, and by the same logic, it takes nothing from us and benefits everyone if we appreciate and wish the best for all others.

If we were to boil down all the reasons people choose to go into negative states rather than resourceful loving states, we would find fear: fear of rejection, fear of loss, fear of not satisfying our needs—basically, a fear that there could be significant pain as a result of being in a loving state. This is an illusion, however, because it is our disconnection with others that causes the biggest and most long-lasting pain of them all. Even those who have radically disconnected themselves from people and eventually take either their own life or the lives of others can often be seen as having made a final desperate attempt to communicate and connect. The Columbine kids and the Unabomber were sending messages that they did want contact with others. If that had not been true, they would have just gone away quietly by themselves or jumped into a hole off a glacier in obscurity.

Remember, love is a boundless emotional resource. Use it liberally.

Chapter 35

Strategy

The word *strategy* can have many different uses and meanings, depending on its context. In this book it has a very special definition. We use this word to talk about a very specific and important human need, and it can be very helpful and empowering for us to recognize it as a need.

When we say we need a strategy, we mean that we need to have *a way of being in the world* (which may include our assumed identity) that is based on the conviction that our behavior, the values we have, and the decisions we make, are correct. Even if we are not achieving at the level we would like or reaching our goals, we may still believe that what we are doing is correct and that it is the environment or something outside our control that is wrong.

On some level we are in agreement with and condone all of our behavior. Whether we overeat, abuse drugs and alcohol, or are a neat freak or an overachieving workaholic, we believe this strategy is satisfying our needs. The truth is, on some level, it *is* satisfying our needs. For the alcoholic, drinking, even to great excess, can provide a state of relaxation that he doesn't normally give himself permission to experience, variety/novelty, interaction (preferably with those who also drink and will validate this vehicle for satisfying needs), or certainty because he knows it will consistently change his state. Being a workaholic may provide significance, love, and validation, even if it is from the boss rather than close family members.

Many of us believe our strategy is our identity—who we are. For example, if I believe that I am a nice person and I do nice things for others, then I can count on the environment to satisfy my needs. People will appreciate me, give me love, significance, or whatever is important to me. The problem is that this is a bit of an incomplete way of looking at things. Being a nice person is an action, not an attribute, and it is subject to change. If you do ninety-nine good things and then do five ordinary or bad things, does that mean you are an ordinary or bad person?

This is a common perception that causes much unnecessary pain. Does being unable to complete some task turn a person into a failure? Does making an error make someone a stupid or careless person? Babies when learning to walk fail miserably for weeks or even months. Their "failures" are essential to build muscles, coordination, and balance How silly would it be to label the baby as a failure and then discourage them from attempting something so obviously beyond their capability? When we talk about tall people, or redheads, we are referring to attributes, whereas making a mistake or doing something funny are activities or actions.

Somewhere between the baby stage and adulthood, we start to believe that things that are embedded in the structure of our language, things that suggest that our external processes (behavior) are equal to our identity, are our attributes. These beliefs can serve us well as a shortcut for deciding what action to take. After all, if I'm a nice person, I already know what to do. If someone asks me for directions, it is unlikely that I will throw an orange at them. Even though actions are not attributes, we find it useful to think and act in these terms in our day-to-day life.

Just as the nice-person label provides an unconscious shortcut to decide on actions that will satisfy needs, we also find leverage in discouraging others from unwanted behavior by threatening to give them a negative label. "Now Johnny, if you don't get good grades, people will think you are a dummy." Little Johnny then begins to study harder. With such practical payoffs, it is easy to stop questioning this equation. If six-year-old Johnny's mom singles out some particular behavior, such as yelling, from the full range of normal six-year-old behavior and starts calling Johnny an annoying little loudmouth, problems may arise. Even though Mom is only trying to discourage unwanted actions, if she keeps calling Johnny a loudmouth, he might eventually agree with that label and begin producing more of the unwanted behavior. If she believes him to be a loudmouth, he may think "She must be right." The child may not be developed enough to emotionally detach and effectively challenge the label completely.

Actions versus attributes is an important distinction, and affects many areas of our lives. Let's walk through another scenario slowly for fullest understanding. Johnny, a normal bright child, would prefer to play video games or watch TV rather than clean and organize his bedroom. This is typical childish behavior. However, if the parent suggests that this preference is due to an attribute of laziness or uncaring, a seed will be planted, and continued statements of this sort will water the idea until it grows in Johnny's mind to the point where he starts believing that he really is lazy and uncaring. He believes it because he now has a justification for watching TV. This "lazy thing" is serving pretty well to satisfy his needs. He has now become more difficult to motivate, and the family and others will get creative and give him all sorts of specific attention and concern that he may perceive as a loving connection.

So, by being a lazy person, he really doesn't have to plan to do anything. Unconsciously he already knows how "lazy people" behave, and most importantly, the behavior works to satisfy several of his needs at high levels.

He has certainty that he can get a response and/or attention. His strategy is validated as he satisfies his needs for variety, significance, and a certain amount of connection from others. If his environment continues to support this strategy, it will be easier for him to become addicted to this pattern—outside of his awareness. A supportive environment by definition makes it easy to satisfy needs, regardless of positive or negative outcomes.

There are other benefits to the behavior, which may help other people. His mother is satisfying some of her own needs: she believes her identity as a mother is even more important because he has a problem that calls to her parenting instincts. Of course she is not intentionally doing something harmful, probably believing she is very close to her children, a primary source of love and connection for her. As a successful mother she feels significant, loved, and validated that her strategy works. This could keep going. Maybe Mom doesn't feel sufficiently loved by her husband or her other children. So she may value the relationship with Johnny a little too much. By having lazy Johnny at home in his room watching TV, she may feel more certainty in her love and connection with him. She may on some level hope that he will not become ambitious and never leave the nest, enabling her to continue her role as mother that satisfies all her needs. Her behavior may also be a safe and indirect way to communicate to her husband that he is not satisfying her needs, a cry for help, if you will. On top of all that, Johnny is creating an alliance to safely satisfy both his and Mom's need for love and connection without the risks that can be associated with an intimate relationship.

With this expanding network of reinforcing behavior, where a number of needs are being met simultaneously, it would be understandable if Johnny continues acting lazy or depressed, and eventually starts drinking or smoking or doing drugs, even if he consciously understands that this unhealthy behavior ultimately will not give him a fulfilling life. The unconscious belief that it works may be the strongest influencer of his actions.

Johnny, now accepting laziness as his own identity, will gravitate towards a peer group that validates laziness as a virtue. It is highly unlikely he would join a group of highly motivated individuals as peers. When we look at groups of kids, we can identify the types of attribute labels that are linked with their strategy for satisfying their needs and acceptance. In any school setting you'll find cliques based on similar value sets, regardless of geography, intelligence, or economic resources: the nerds, the popular kids, the ones into music, the jocks, the rebels. While these are all different types of behavior, they are all designed to satisfy similar or even identical needs.

Were you told as a child that you were a good girl, or a goof-off, or a deep thinker? What effect did that have on you? Did you accept that identity/attribute, or did you rebel and embrace a different strategy? If so, was that different strategy based on an identity that you believed would satisfy all your needs at high levels? Did you believe that your environment required you to be someone you were not to satisfy your emotional needs? This, of course, is very common, because parents, grandparents, teachers, and friends often withhold approval or positive emotions in an attempt to leverage us into a behavior more aligned with their own strategy.

The behaviors you engage in now in this part of your life are a direct reflection of the strategy you have adopted to satisfy your needs. Whether this strategy was due to your conforming with or rebelling against others, their behavior toward you has had a profound effect on your strategy. Your top two needs will have had a dramatic effect on your life. A person who values love and variety the most will have a very different life from a person who values certainty and significance. Likewise, different strategies will be associated with different vehicles that we use to satisfy the needs we value most. Take significance. Our identity as a lazy person will allow us to be significant through the awe we inspire in others by breezing through life never really doing anything. Quite impressive, really. A high achiever may find significance by repeatedly making shrewd business decisions. Equally impressive. Same need, different strategies and vehicles.

So what do you need to do, and how do you need to be, to satisfy your needs? Are you an achiever, a comedian, a worrier or a warrior, a warm friend or a distanced observer? What strategic needs will these vehicles of identity satisfy? Are the identity vehicles satisfying them well in your current situation, or were they set up in a totally different environment and today are useless?

Strategies that are brought down to the level of identity/attribute tend to be used cross-contextually, that is to say, in all areas of our lives, and this can have certain consequences. Being a sharp, logical, and suspicious person can be excellent in the context of being a detective interviewing a witness. However, it will cause interesting challenges back at home at the dinner table, where a kinder, gentler strategy is called for. Being a damsel in distress may provide an opportunity for your prince to make a well-timed rescue, saving you and living with you happily ever after. However, when the damsel is in continual distress, in spite of your capable prince's efforts, he will feel like a failure and seek to satisfy his needs through other relationships or vehicles.

Some strategies no longer work in any context. The depressed drug addict son who previously had, through his addictive behavior, felt his need for variety to be very high (no pun intended) had also been led to feel validated, connected with others, and perhaps loved by concerned family members. He felt certain he could change his state any time he took the drugs. He had a significant problem that no one could solve, which of course guaranteed an ongoing vehicle.

However, at some point his family has disowned him and refuses contact. He is unable to maintain deep or meaningful relationships with many people because his peers are entirely self-focused as well or they have moved on in their life to a new stage. He is unemployable, and most groups of people would consider him a drain on their system and therefore prevent his membership or access. The systems in which he could satisfy his needs with other people would be hospitals, prisons, or drug rehab, so his alternative is to collect disability and lay low, self-validating his limiting strategy among a similar peer group. Because he associates satisfying his needs with the identity of being a drug addict, he feels a connection with it that is stronger than any chemical addiction to drugs themselves. When a person is in therapy or treatment that does not treat or recognize this class of issue, the person will be more prone to relapse than if treatment had intervened on these levels and made the appropriate changes in their strategy.

As I have said, your strategy can be understood as your opinion of how you need to be to satisfy your needs. The truth is, however, that there is no one fixed way to satisfy all your needs in every context, and certainly not in all the inevitable various stages of your life. In the same way that it is better to put your ego aside, it is also better to put your strategy in its proper place. It is a servant to you, a flexible servant that can easily adjust to use the proper vehicles to satisfy your needs and the needs of those closest to you in positive ways. At a core level, your strategy has the highest intentions for you. You are a good person and you are capable of supporting others and doing great things yourself.

Sometimes we believe our environment prevents us from being our core selves and we censor ourselves and our behavior. The truth is, a woman who has a radiant presence serves herself and the world better by allowing herself to experience what is within her consistently. Similarly, a man who is a strong good man, is in reality even stronger and more appreciated when he lives from his core beliefs in his heart as to what is right.

You need to apply the same thinking and rules to others. You must recognize that no matter how brilliant your strategy is, it does not mean that everyone else should adopt the same values and strategy. Everyone has a right to satisfy their needs in the way they choose, especially if they are not harming anyone else. It is true that with your understanding, you may be able to assist people in using better vehicles.

Giving you the tools to change a bad strategy to a good strategy is definitely one of the goals of this book. Explaining that directly in the simplest of terms will have obvious benefits. So here goes.

Whether it is you or someone else, you must be aware of the needs that the strategy is fulfilling, and understand that needs are desired emotional targets that we are taking action towards. That action occurs regardless of the overall destructive or beneficial effect.

When you know what the needs are and, furthermore, embrace them as values, you can find appropriate vehicles based on context and goals to reach those emotional targets. Make sure that the vehicles are good for you and others, feel good for you as you do them, and support the greater good long-term.

As you use these vehicles for a time and directly empower yourself to experience achieving the emotional targets, your unconscious process will begin to take over and create habits around your new positive vehicles. Given the choice of a negative vehicle that you are emotionalized against versus a positive vehicle that you are emotionalized toward, unconsciously you will move in the positive direction.

Lastly, remember to make a goal of being, and staying, fulfilled. Use a combination of desirable long-term goals that can be updated, upon their completion, in a way appropriate to your life stage. Combine these with daily goals that allow you to satisfy your emotional targets, and medium-range goals that keep the medium-range horizon appealing and worthwhile. By doing this, you can find ongoing fulfillment in complete harmony with your environment.

The End

Lynn Cross has been a word lover her entire life and an editor for many years.
See her website: www.wingsforyourwords.com. She writes effective promotion and publicity materials, and is a creative writer too—poetry, stories, memoir, and a newspaper column. She is a performer and producer for the Wild Yam Cabaret (www.wildyamcabaret.org) and has appeared in the Minnesota Fringe, Balls Cabaret, West End Arts, and others. She often mentors aspiring storytellers and poets. Her theater background ensures that she is always sensitive to the all-important. . . *audience!* In terms of the world at large, she is conversant with a wide range of fields, but her area of greatest expertise is the social sciences, especially personality and social psychology. She has a B.A. in English and psychology from the University of Minnesota, and an A.B.D. (all but dissertation) in experimental social psychology and child development from Cornell University.

Front cover illustration

Hugh Bennewitz is an Illustrator, Graphic Designer and Mural Painter living and working in Minnetonka, Minnesota. He graduated from the Minneapolis College of Art and Design.
Email- hugh.bennewitz@gmail.com

Rear cover illustration and all interior illustrations

Michael Beachy illustrator, St. Paul, MN. He was trained in Printmaking, Painting, and Illustration, first at the Perpich Center of Art Education and later at Emily Carr Institute of Art and Design. He has designed and painted some 13 murals, and self published two small artist books. He also maintains an art blog. You can view it at http://benchyboy.blogspot.com his portfolio at http://cargocollective.com/thebenchy/ and contact him for commissions through his email msenseab@gmail.com